Vivian Maier

Introduction by Anne Morin

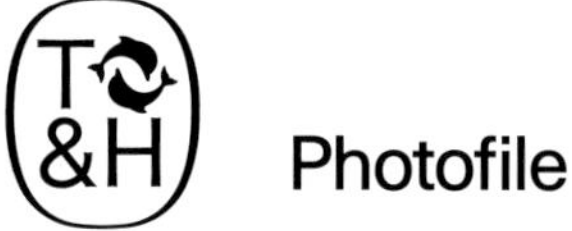

Photofile

A life in the shadows

The history of the world is not always written in a linear way, as it is woven. Sometimes, perhaps because the moment is right, history changes course. It doubles back and returns along the same path to uncover forgotten territory. It retraces its formerly hurried footsteps and wanders into the shadows, into unknown worlds that may hold vast looming continents.

This was the case for Vivian Maier, the unknown woman who may just as well have spent her life in silence: a sketch of a face, a story that faded almost as it was being written.

Ms. Maier, perceived in life as a nanny or childminder, is now "Vivian Maier, photographer," a grand figure who sits within the history of photography alongside the greatest names of the 20th century. Although fate pushed her into the shadows in life, she now stands like a monolith, next to Diane Arbus, Henri Cartier-Bresson, Robert Frank, Robert Doisneau, Helen Levitt, and those yet to come.

Born in New York in 1926, to a French mother, Maria Jaussaud, and a father with Austro-Hungarian roots, Charles von Maier, Vivian spent her early years in a gloomy home with quarreling parents. In the early 1930s, the relationship between Charles and Maria reached breaking point. Maria took her daughter and went to live in the Bronx, in the home of a close friend, Jeanne Bertrand, a renowned artist and photographer. Then came a long series of journeys between New York and the valley of Champsaur in the French Alps, where she spent part of her childhood.

In the late 1940s, she began to be interested in photography and took her first pictures, armed with a Kodak Brownie camera that apparently belonged to her mother. Portraits and landscapes were her favorite subjects. She collected these on long walks, going where the pathways took her, between fields and valleys, from one village to the next. These photographs are fascinating evidence of the origins of her visual language and the traits that became constituent elements of her style.

Vivian Maier was self-taught and her status as an amateur photographer gave her the freedom to invent her own visual language. She developed it steadfastly and diligently from the 1950s onward, first moving to New York in 1951, then Chicago in 1956, until the early 1990s. Her entire archive is estimated to contain almost 150,000 images and 300 Super 8 and 16 mm films, which is considerable for an amateur photographer.

Within American society, in its most organic aspects, Vivian Maier painstakingly observed the urban fabric that reflected major social and political changes. This was the age of the American Dream, of an overemphasis on hegemony and modernity, but it was its flipside that went on to become the very essence of Vivian Maier's work. She captured it in photographs and on film, creating a visual language that combined humanist photography—a sensibility she owed to her French origins—and American street photography. Street scenes, sidewalk anecdotes, portraits, self-portraits, gestures, and details: these became the checkerboard of Vivian Maier's time. The making of her images was simple, precise, rigorous, and extremely efficient.

The street is a good place for observation, especially the working-class neighborhoods where Vivian Maier constantly wandered. She became part of this human geography in motion, skilfully mastering its choreography and fluctuations. The scenes she photographed were often quirks, anecdotes, coincidences, moments in public life that nobody pays attention to, but she turned them into the subjects of stories through photography. She photographed the sidelines, "that which is generally not taken note of, that which is not noticed, that which has no importance; what happens when nothing happens other than the weather, people, cars, and clouds."[1] Each of her images came from the precise place where reality becomes elusive and fleeting shadows pass before our eyes. It's at this moment that a metamorphosis of reality occurs, the phenomenon Pierre Mac Orlan called the "social fantastic,"[2] the emergence of the extraordinary.

Childhood is a place of illusion ("this last word means nothing less than beginning a game: in-lusio"[3]), appearances and disappearances, dizziness and disequilibrium, giddiness and pretense, a place where vision plays tricks and we allow it to happen. "A poet," Andrei Tarkovsky wrote, "has the imagination and psychology of a child, for his impressions of the world are immediate, however profound his ideas about the world may be.... The poet does not use 'descriptions' of the world; he himself has a hand in its creation."[4] Vivian Maier, in her daily life as a nanny surrounded by children, was able to look at life with the same acuity, and her imagination, "the queen of the faculties,"[5] always remained sharp.

For almost forty years, Vivian Maier was part of the lives of the children she cared for. Attentive to the tiniest details, she photographed their faces, the canvas of their emotions, their expressions and their gazes, their games and their make-believe, a neverending source of inspiration. When she wandered through the streets of New York and Chicago, she got as close as she could to see better. She would pause on a face, photograph it like holding up a mirror. She was attracted by those who, like her, were invisible; those who don't appear anywhere because they're relegated to the margins of the world. These portraits of those forgotten by the American dream speak of poverty, hard work, and suffering. They speak of dark fates that should not be spoken of. Vivian Maier photographs these austere and impassive faces, frontally and without warning, before they can pose. She does not snatch their image but restores some of their dignity. Sometimes, she strays from this rule and wittily photographs high-class ladies, squeezed into their garish outfits. Vivian Maier seems to enjoy intimidating them, suddenly appearing in front of them with her imposing stature.

She is also being playful when she scatters clues to her presence in her self-portraits, which punctuate her photographic journey. She uses different visual techniques to suggest it, including shadows, silhouettes, reflections, and images within images. She adapts this vocabulary to suit the situation and plays around with its elements to assert her existence. Sometimes the clues are only a discreet allusion, a tip of the hat to those who know where to look. They can also be an undeniable affirmation that she herself is the subject of the image.

In one way or another, self-representation or self-portrait, allusion or declaration of intent, Vivian Maier invites the viewer to play a guessing game but the solution always remains a mystery.

Unlike Narcissus who drowned in self-contemplation, Vivian Maier's interest in self-portraits seems more like a necessary quest for her own identity. Reduced to invisibility by her social status and condition, she discreetly and silently establishes irrefutable proof of her presence in a world where she seemed to have no place.

The cast shadow, which became the hallmark of her self-portraits, is characterized by being connected to a body, a doubled body—"every visible is cut out in the tangible"[6]—that has the ability to make the absent present. The shadow attests to the existence of a referent, yet it simultaneously erases its presence. The self-portrait becomes like "the other" in the writings of Emmanuel Levinas, a "third person presence [that] exactly indicates the simultaneity of that presence and that absence."[7]

On her urban wanderings, Vivian Maier was interested in those removed from the frenetic pace of the street, those who existed in a kind of suspended space-time, those who were waiting, watching, or pacing. This latency creates a space in which the fantastic can arise. From it, Vivian Maier collects all kinds of clues—gestures, postures, and attitudes—like a form of domestic archaeology. These people seem to be witnesses to something imminent that is about to occur and that only they can see in this strange atmosphere, suspended between two worlds. Hands are often the central motifs in these images; they unwittingly speak life into those to whom they belong. Vivian Maier photographs fleeting gestures, like reflexes, automatic motions that betray the workings of the unconscious. Each of the gestures she catalogues is the starting point of a statement, a story yet to happen.

Vivian Maier continued to view the world in close-up. She cast her gaze into uninhabited spaces, took close-ups of details and objects that she observed with such intensity that they lose their substance and seem stripped of narrative content. She strips down forms, depleting them until the bond that connects these images to their referent is stretched so thin that they topple into abstraction.

These photographs are a sort of documentary record whose only endpoint is accumulation and sedimentation, building up a living, organic layered matrix of the world.

This practice brings to mind the ragpicker, a street collector who sorts through the detritus of the age. The ragpicker remains one of the most symbolic figures of Paris under the Second Empire. Baudelaire sketched the following portrait, which could almost be that of Vivian Maier: "Here is a man whose task it is to pick up all the rubbish produced on one day in the capital. All that the great city has thrown out, all it has lost, all it has disdained, all it has broken, he catalogues and collects. He consults the archives of debauchery, works through the lumber room of rubbish. He makes a selection, chooses astutely; he picks up, as a miser seizes on treasure, the refuse which, when chewed over by the divinity of industry, will become objects of use and enjoyment. […] He arrives, wagging his head and stumbling over the cobbles like those young poets who spend all their days wandering around in search of rhymes. He is talking to himself; he pours out his soul to the dark cold night air."[8] The ragpicker's rebellion, like that of Vivian Maier, seems to be hopeless in the face of the society that rejects them. They have no other choice than to recognize in detritus "the face that the world of things turns directly and solely to them."[9]

If we remember that Vivian Maier's body of work grew by moving from one theme to another like crossing the boundary of a territory only to keep coming back, there is nonetheless a specific point at which her language condenses, like a center of gravity powered by a confluence of different sources: color photography, film, and the alternation between the fixed image and "the movement-image,"[10] which could be called kineticism. These three areas are interconnected and lead to a more experimental pathway.

In the late 1950s, Vivian Maier moved in with the Gensburg family, on the shores of Lake Michigan. This is when a change in her photographic language occurred. She embraced color and her images resounded with it. Images became music, sight became hearing. When we look at her color images of Chicago streets, we can hear the beat of the urban landscape, the rhythm of the blues. Through nothing more than a juxtaposition of tones, she creates an echo, and the image becomes a colorful game in which color itself is the protagonist.

By then she was using a Leica 35 mm, very different from the square format Rolleiflex that she used to take most of her black and white shots. The rectangular format added a certain dynamism to the composition, rather like that of filmmaking, with which she was experimenting at the same time. Her relationship with time began to change and motion became part of her work. Vivian Maier played with timescales by creating sequences of motion, as if transposing the specifics of the language of film into the photographic image. She made use of fragmentation and repetition to simulate movement, and simultaneity to indicate displacement and duration. She created cinematic sequences using the twelve shots from her Rolleiflex camera, evoking a filmic sense of the linear progression of space-time. This period went on to be fundamental in the evolution of her work, because it marked a crossing point between two languages, which continued to display ongoing correspondences.

In the mid-1960s, she began to make films with an 8 mm or 16 mm camera, filmed frontally, with no tricks or editing. Her films tell us not only about the locations she filmed, but also about her way of seeing. In a way, they render visible the shifting of her gaze, her movements through space, and take on the form of an experimental documentary. Film became a tool that came before the photograph. In fact, during this period, Vivian Maier took both her Super 8 camera and her Rolleiflex on her urban excursions. She would start with film as if it were an exercise in looking, searching for a photographic image; as soon as one appeared, she swapped cine film for photographic film and captured it. Vivian Maier possessed the ability to anticipate and foresee. Her intuition allowed her to wait and let these miraculous moments occur.

Shortly before her death in 2009, Vivian Maier's archive was discovered by chance at an auction. Her work then began its slow rise to the surface of visibility, eventually making her one of the most fascinating photographers of the 20th century.

Vivian Maier, as Rilke said of Rodin, "seized upon the life that was everywhere about [her]. [She] grasped it in its smallest details; [she] observed it and it followed [her]; [she] awaited it at the crossroads where it lingered; [she] overtook it as it ran before [her], and [she] found it in all places equally great, equally powerful and overwhelming."[11] The discovery of her work has given a second life to Vivian Maier. It is never too late to set history right by retracing its path.

Anne Morin

Notes

1. Georges Perec, *An Attempt at Exhausting a Place in Paris* (1983), trans. Marc Lowenthal, Cambridge, MA: Wakefield Press, 2010.
2. Pierre Mac Orlan, "La photographie et le fantastique social," *Écrits sur la photographie*, Paris: Textuel, 2011, pp. 59–64.
3. Roger Caillois, *Man, Play, and Games* (1958), trans. Meyer Barash, Urbana and Chicago: University of Illinois Press, 2001, p. 19.
4. Andrei Tarkovsky, *Sculpting in Time: Reflections on the Cinema*, trans. Kitty Hunter-Blair, Austin: University of Texas Press, 2003, pp. 41–42.
5. Charles Baudelaire, "The Salon of 1859," from *The Mirror of Art: Critical Studies by Baudelaire*, trans. Jonathan Mayne, London: Phaidon, 1955.
6. Maurice Merleau-Ponty, *The Visible and the Invisible*, ed. Claude Lefort, trans. Alfonso Lingis, Evanston, IL: Northwestern University Press, 1968, p. 134.
7. Emmanuel Levinas, "The I and the Totality," in *Entre Nous: On Thinking-of-the-Other*, trans. Michael B. Smith and Barbara Harshav, New York: Columbia University Press, 1998, p. 30
8. Charles Baudelaire, *On Wine and Hashish* (1851), London: Hesperus Press, 2002.
9. Walter Benjamin, *One-Way Street and Other Writings*, trans. Edmund Jephcott and Kingsley Shorter, London: NLB, 1979, p. 53.
10. Gilles Deleuze, *Cinema 1: The Movement-Image*, trans. Hugh Tomlinson and Barbara Habberjam, Minneapolis: University of Minnesota Press, 1986.
11. Rainer Maria Rilke, *Auguste Rodin*, trans. Jessie Lemont and Hans Trausil, New York: Sunrise Turn Inc., 1919.

1. New York, 1953.

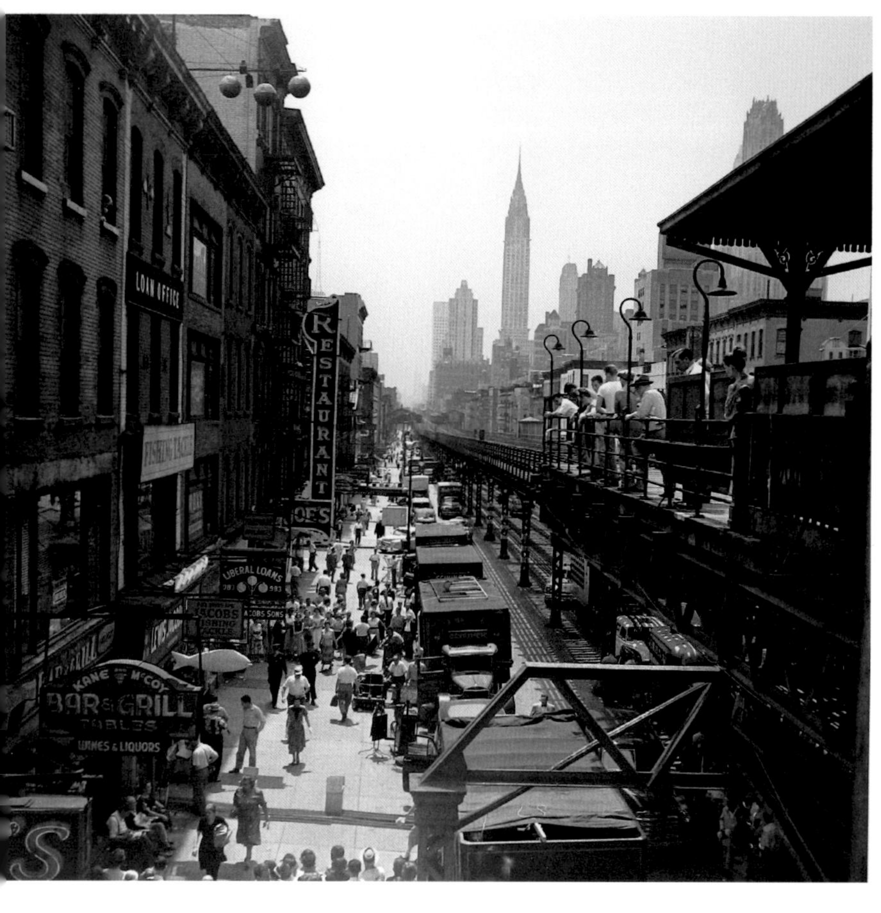

2. New York, 1954.

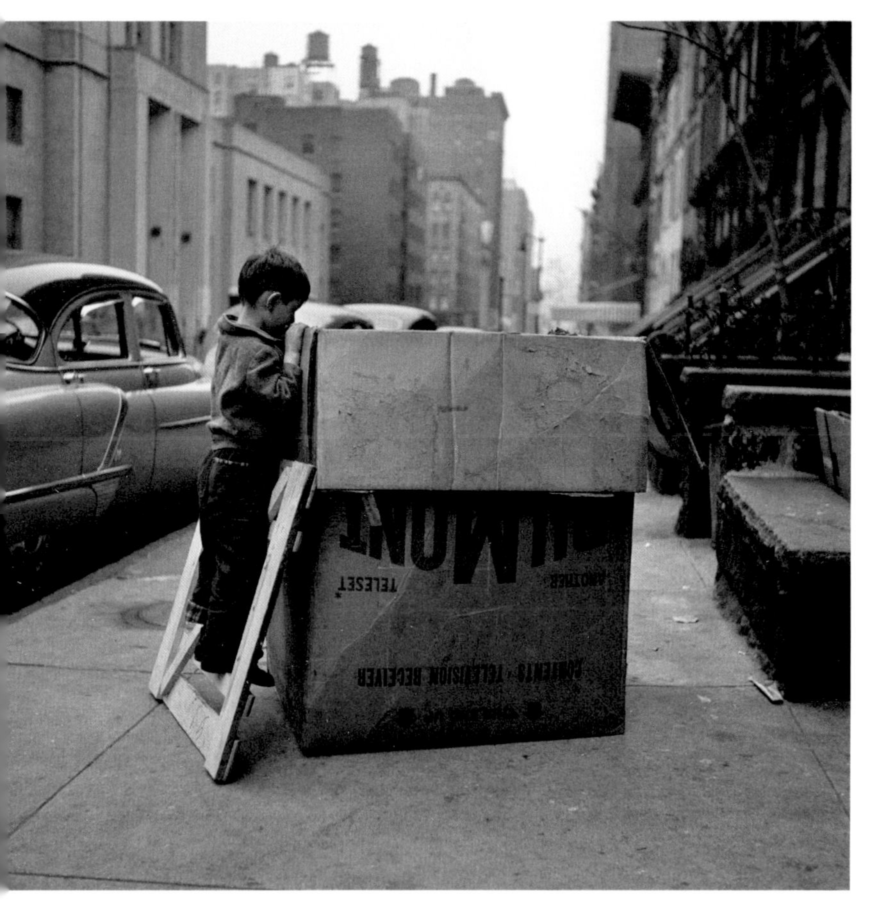

DUMONT
ANOTHER * TELESET
CONTENTS · TELEVISION RECEIVER

3. New York, March 1953.

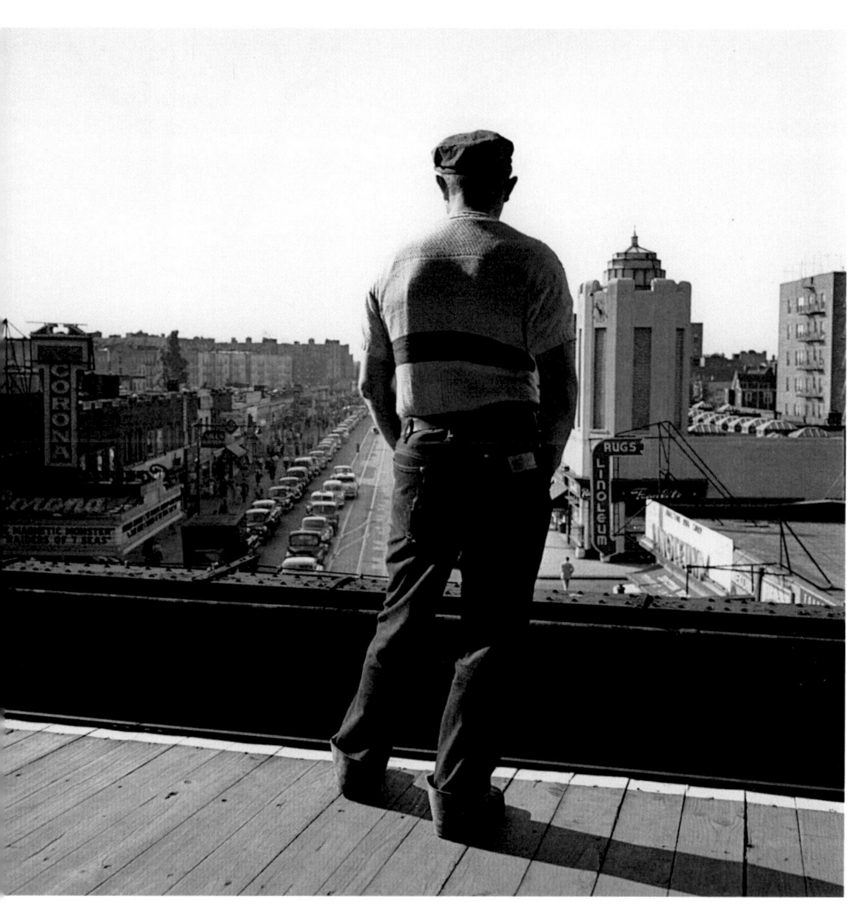

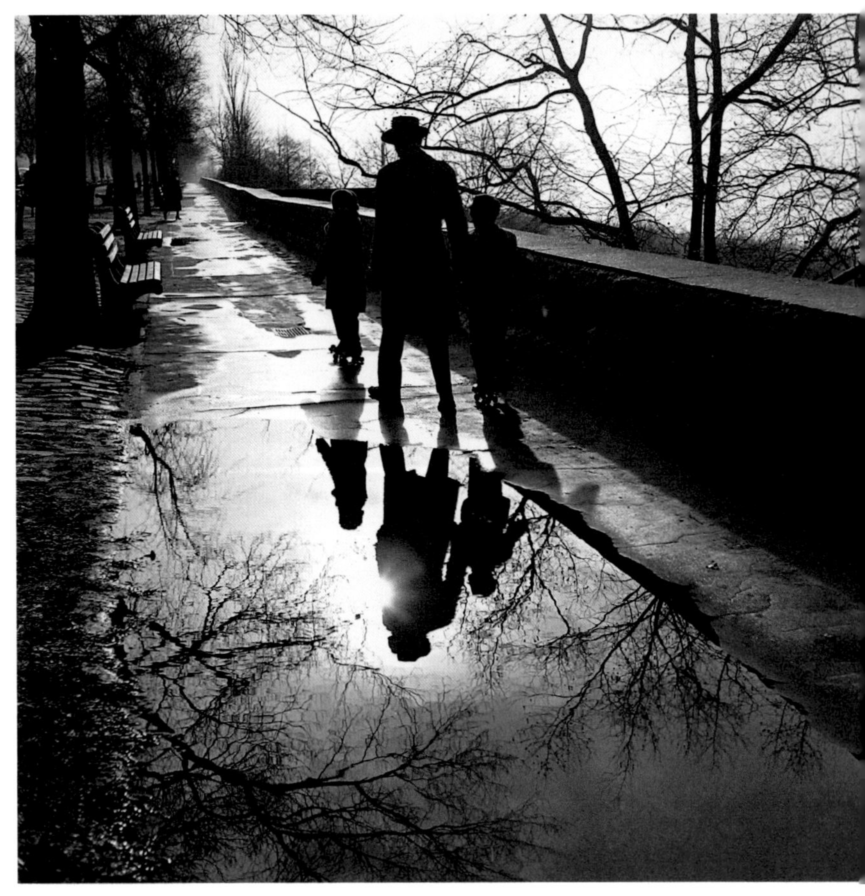

4. New York, January 1953.
5. New York, October 31, 1954.

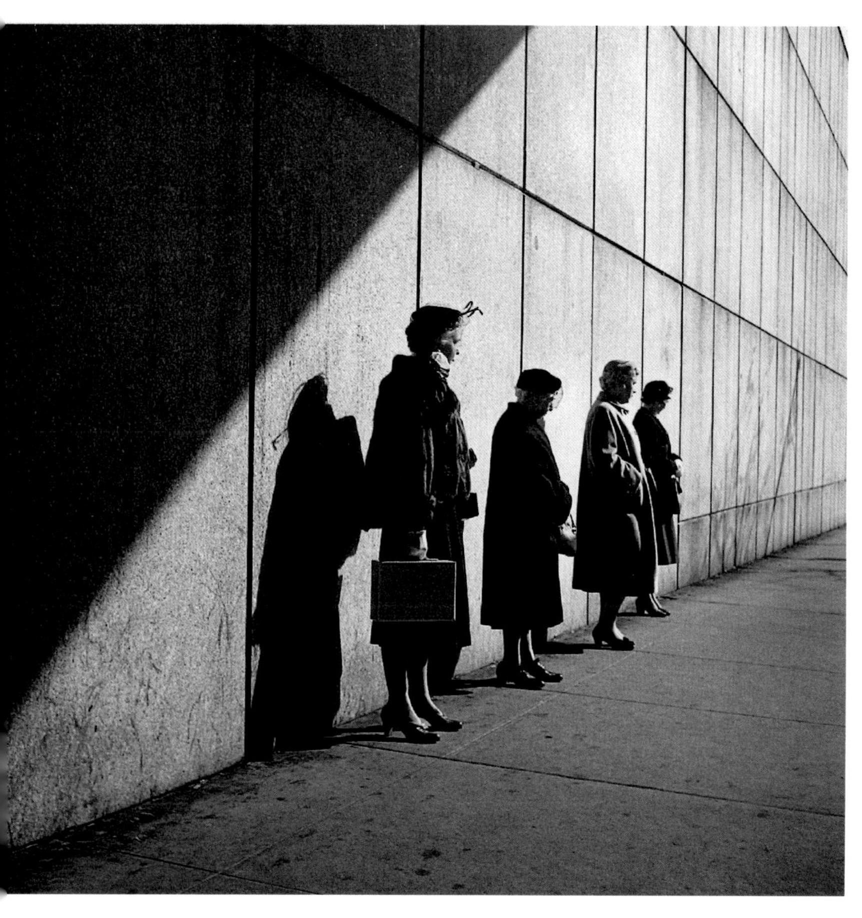

6. Chicago, ca. 1960.

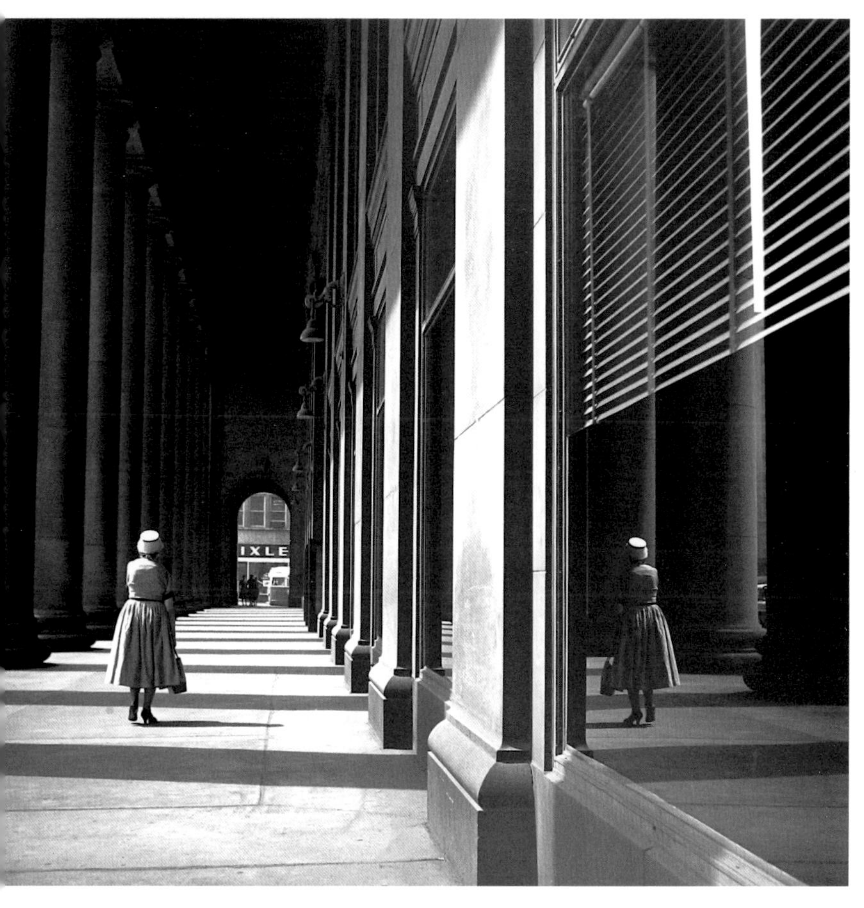
IXLE

7. Self-portrait, train to Los Angeles, 1959.

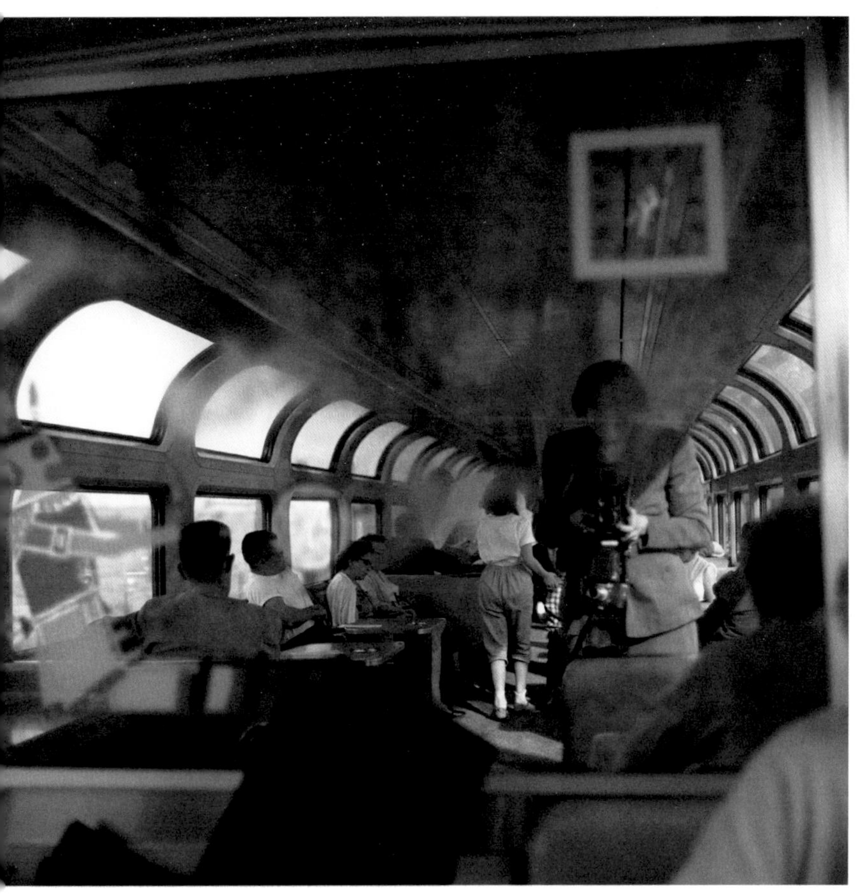

8. New York, August 12, 1954.

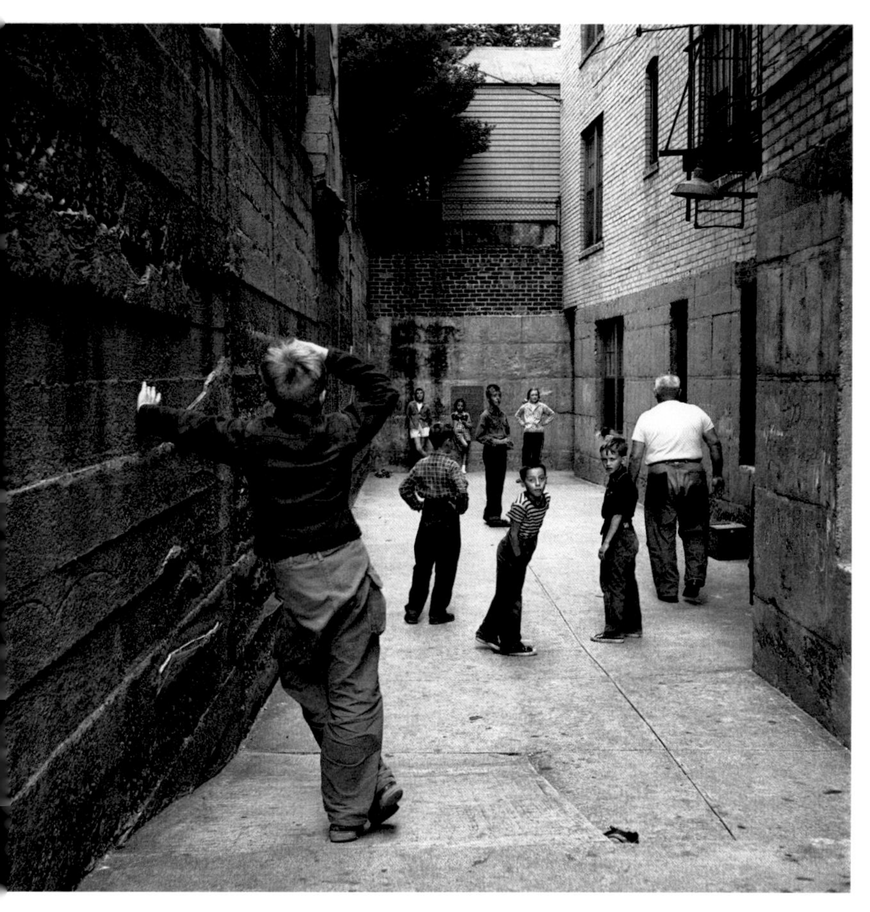

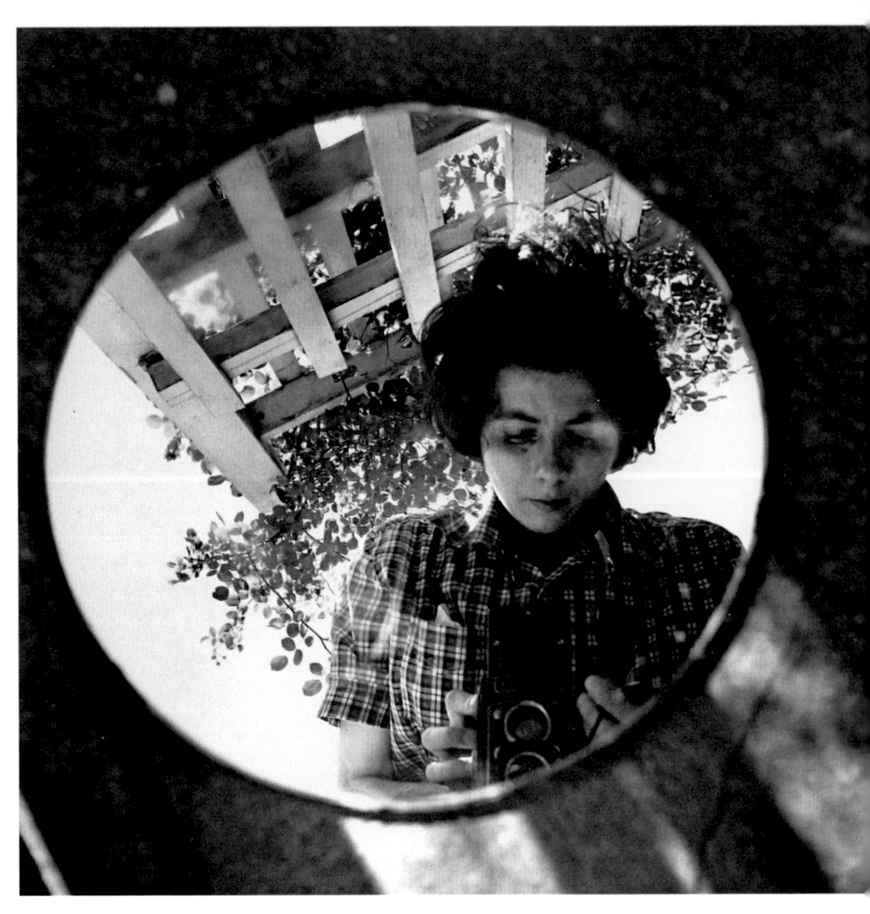

9. Self-portrait, New York, 1953.
10. New York, 1953.

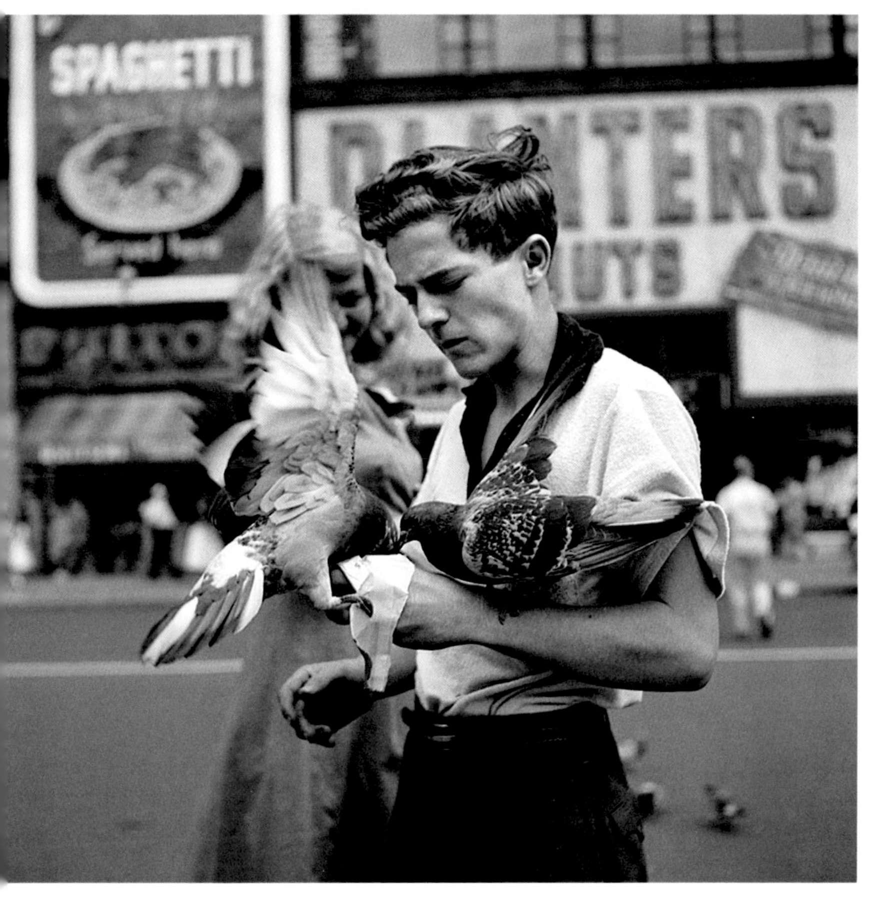

SPAGHETTI
PLANTERS
NUTS

11. Self-portrait, New York, 1955.

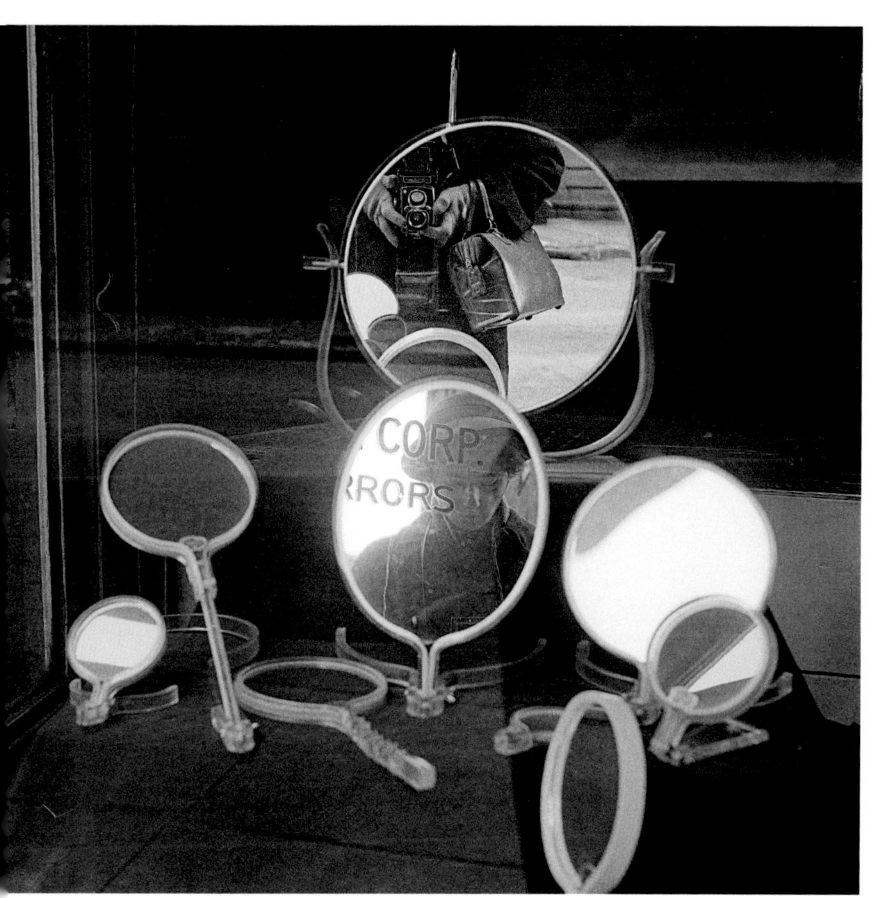
CORP.
RRORS

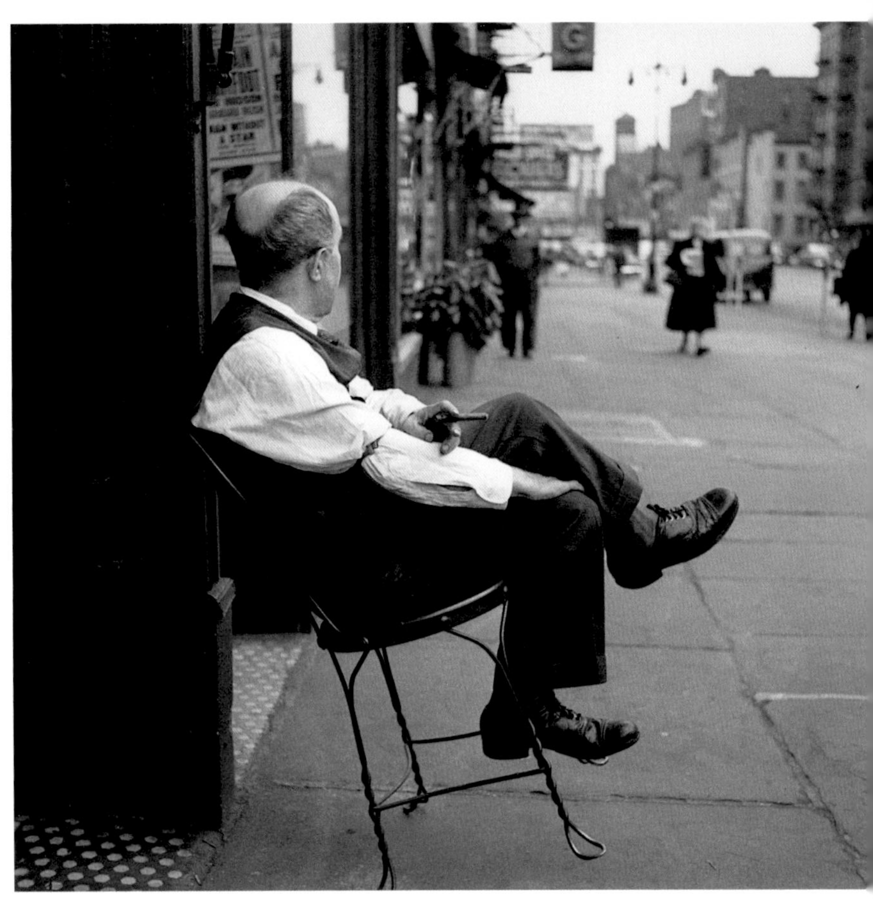

12. New York, 1956.

13. Chicago, 1971.

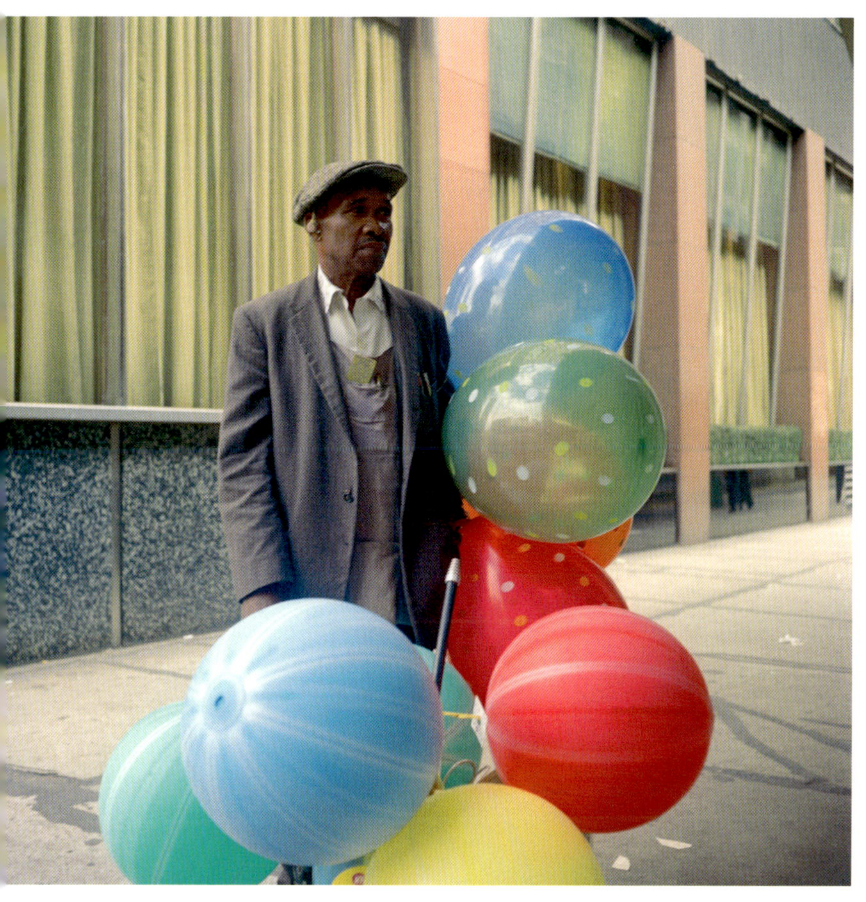

14. Chicago, 1962.

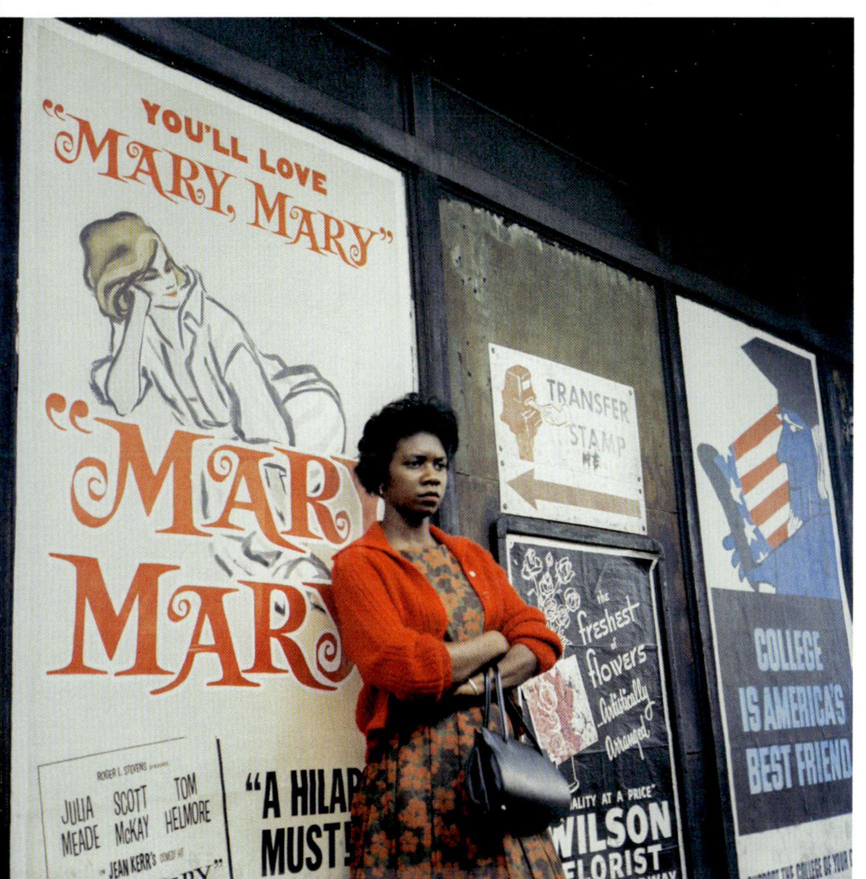
YOU'LL LOVE
"MARY, MARY"
"MARY
MARY
ROGER L. STEVENS presents
JULIA SCOTT TOM
MEADE McKAY HELMORE
"JEAN KERR'S comedy hit
MARY"
"A HILARI
MUST!
TRANSFER
STAMP
HE
the
freshest
of
flowers
...Artistically
Arranged!
QUALITY AT A PRICE"
WILSON
FLORIST
BROADWAY
COLLEGE
IS AMERICA'S
BEST FRIEND
SUPPORT THE COLLEGE OF YOUR

15. New York.

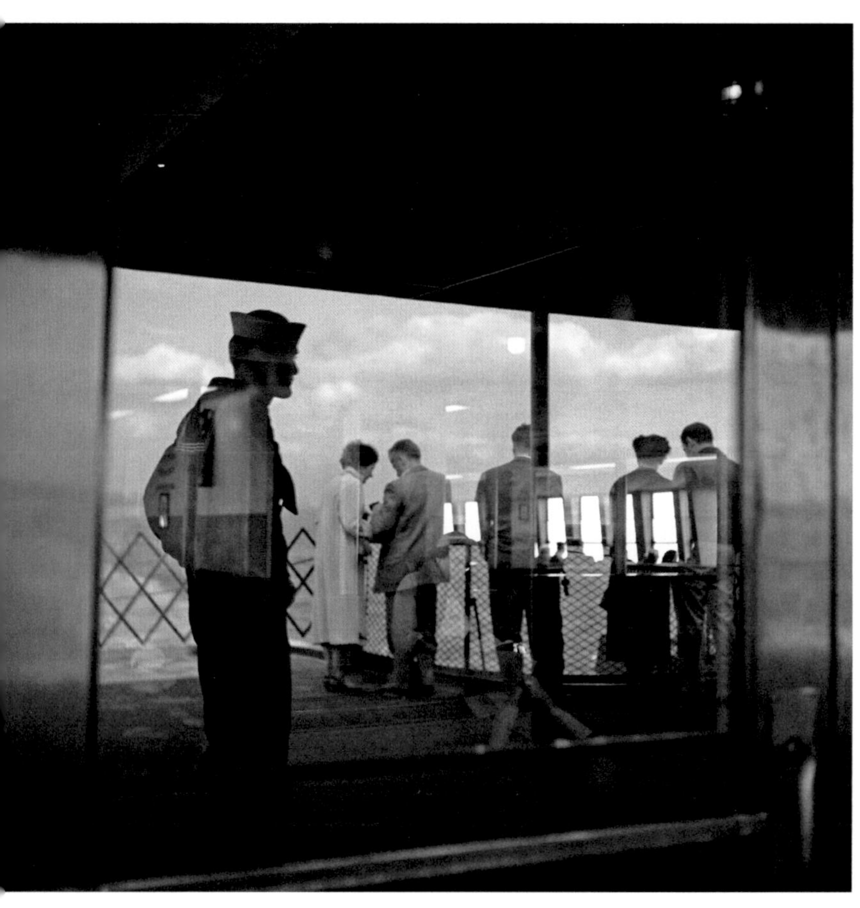

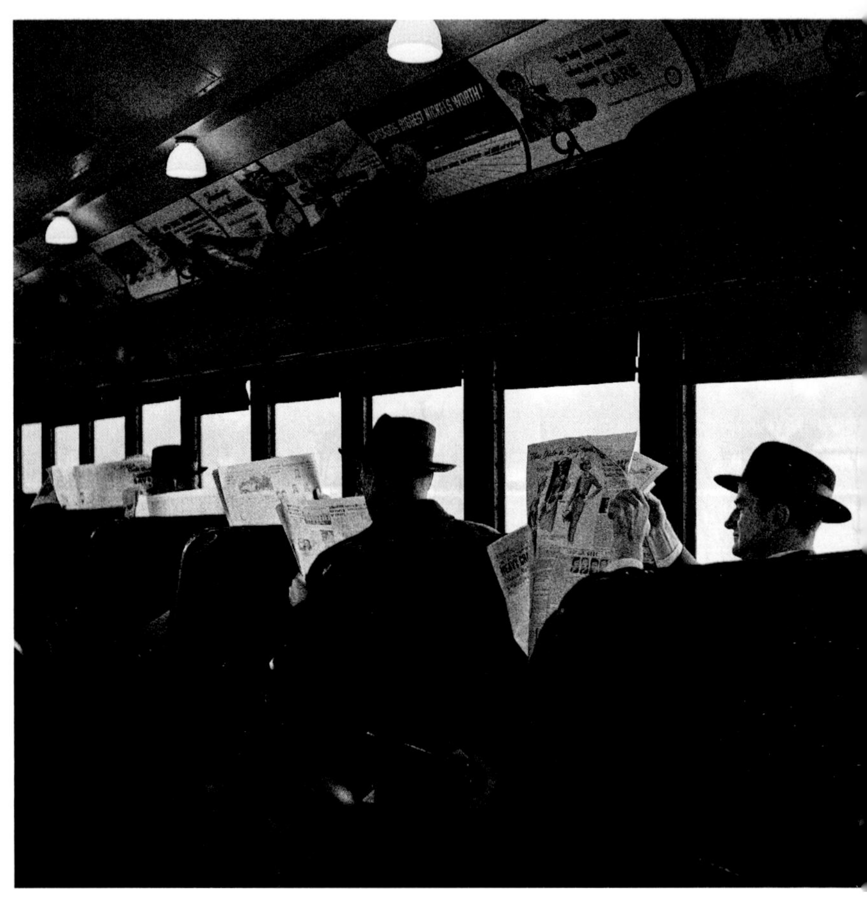

16. Chicago, 1957.

17. Staten Island, New York, June 23, 1954.

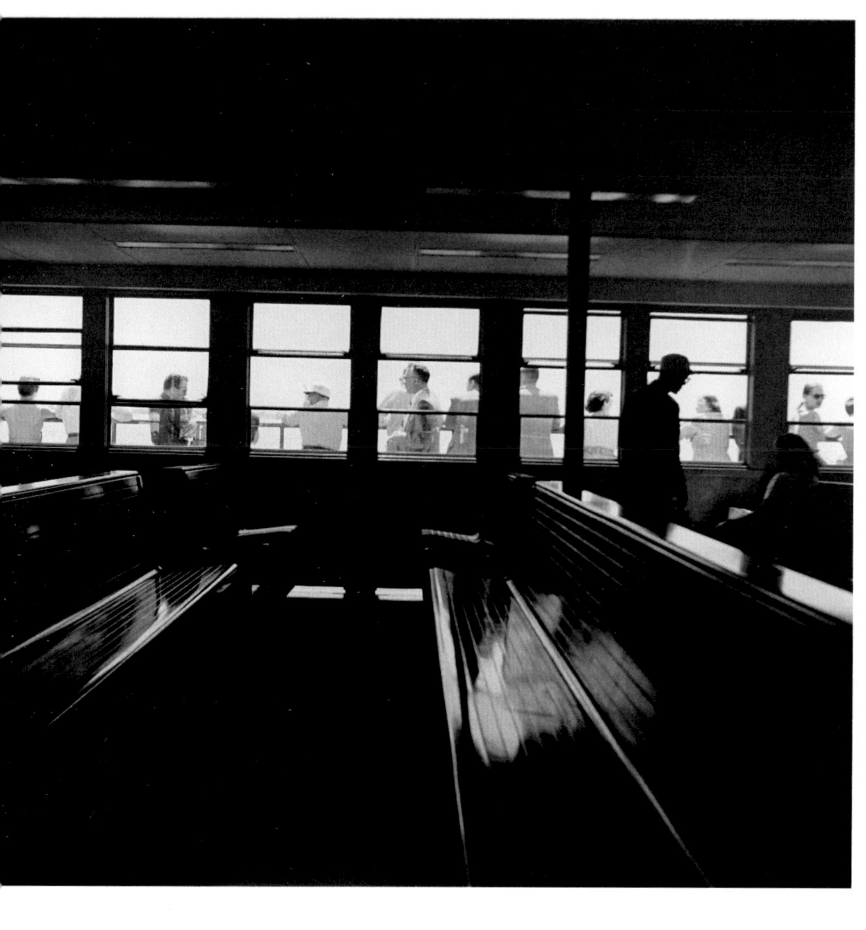

18. Self-portrait, New York, 1954.

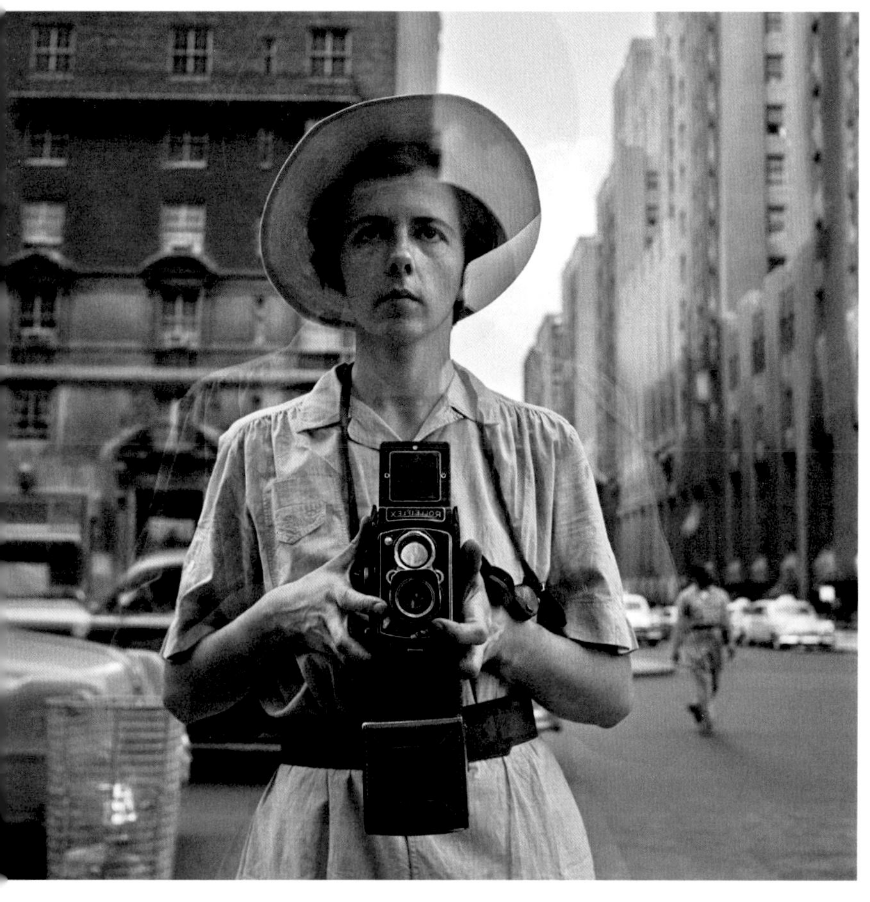

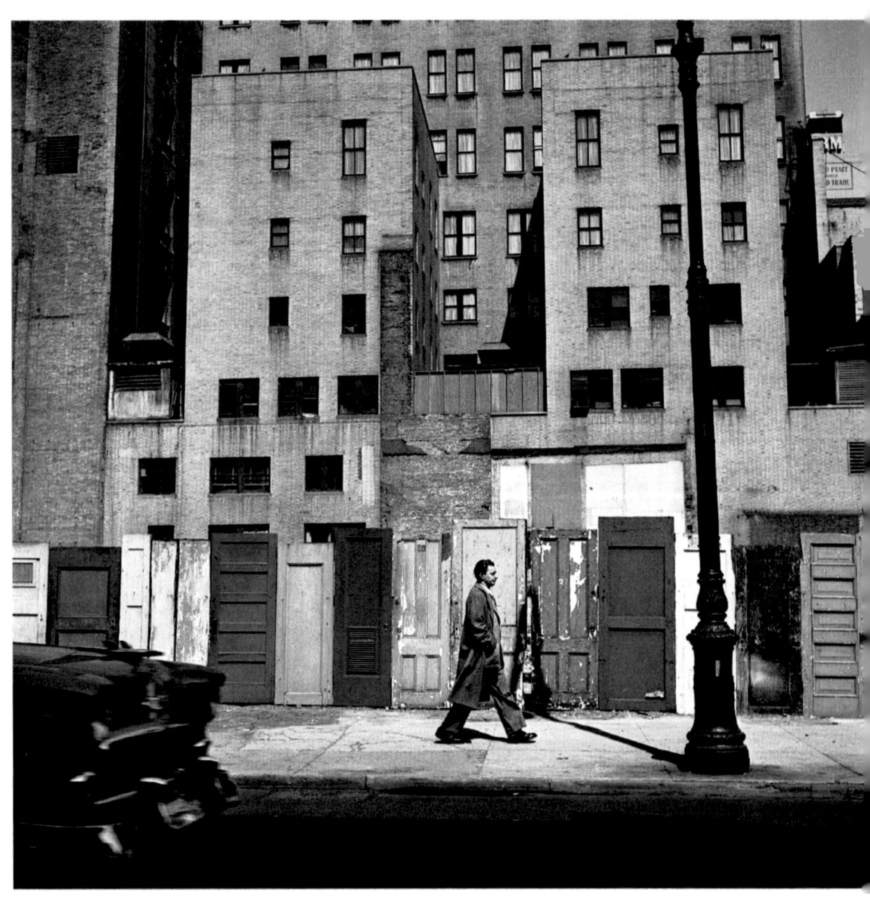

19. New York, ca. 1953.
20. Canada, 1958.

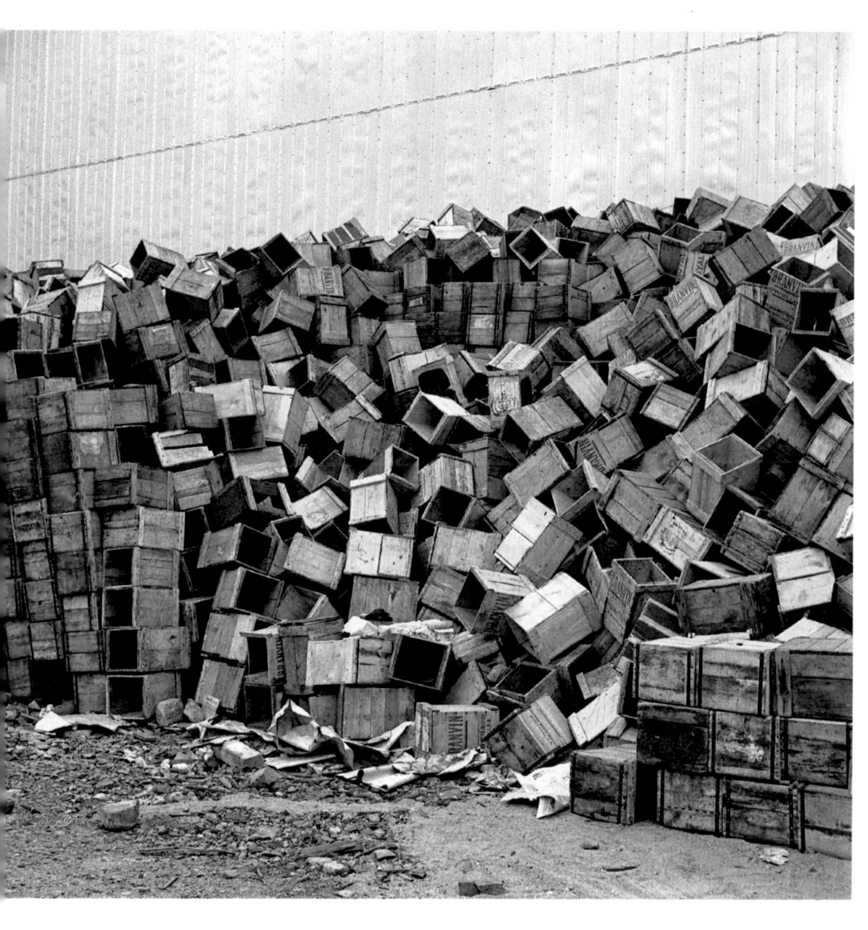

21. New York, 1954.

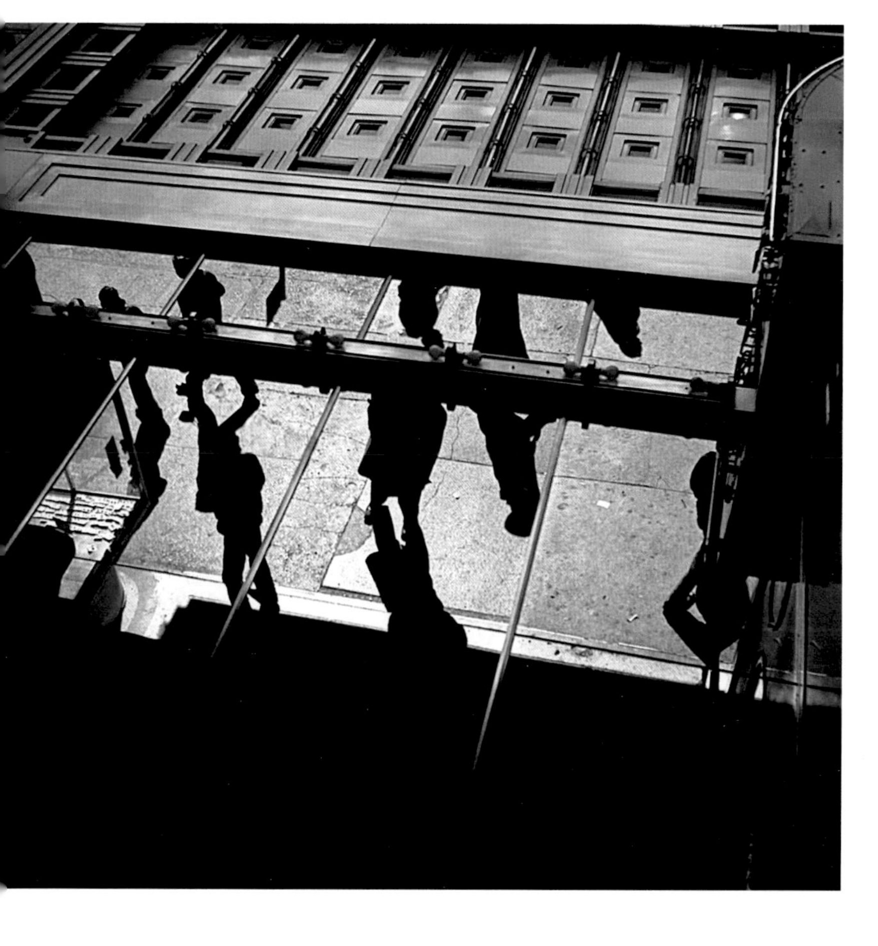

22. Self-portrait, 1956.

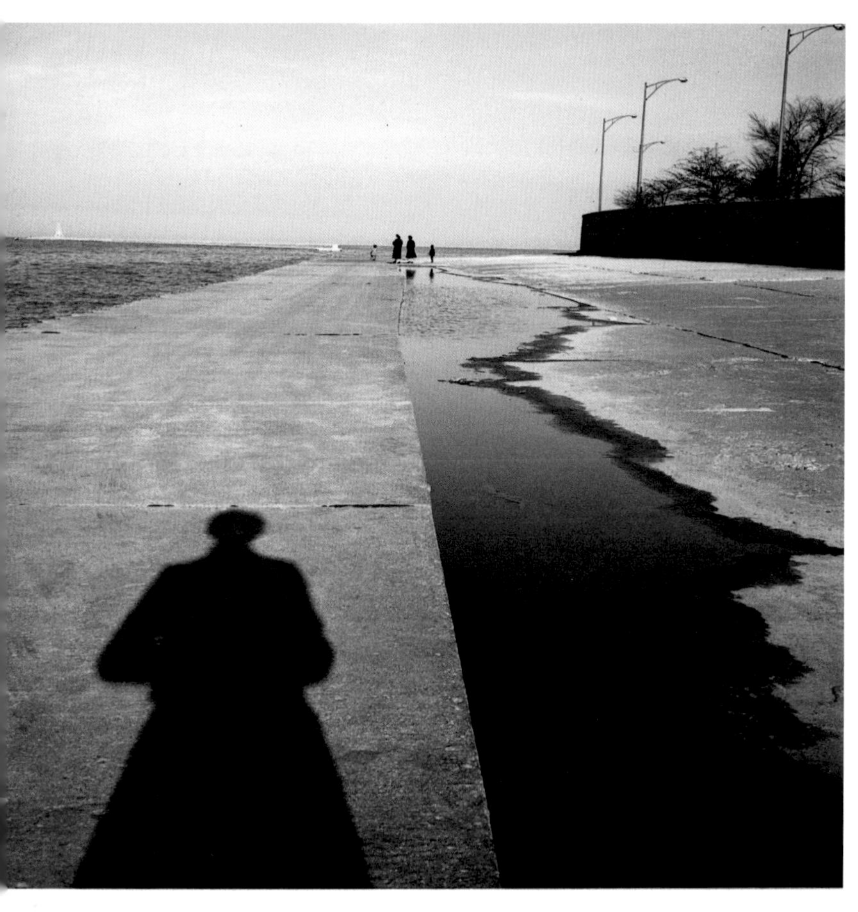

23. Location and date unknown.

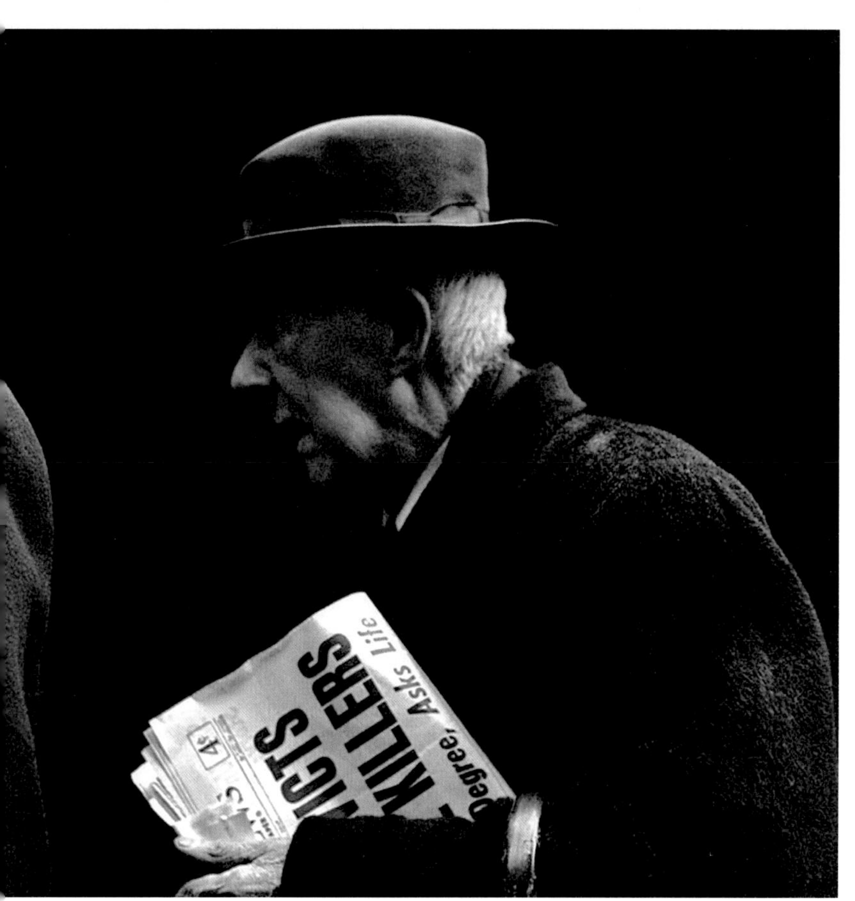

ACTS
KILLERS Life
Degree, Asks
4¢

24. Chicago, May 16, 1957.

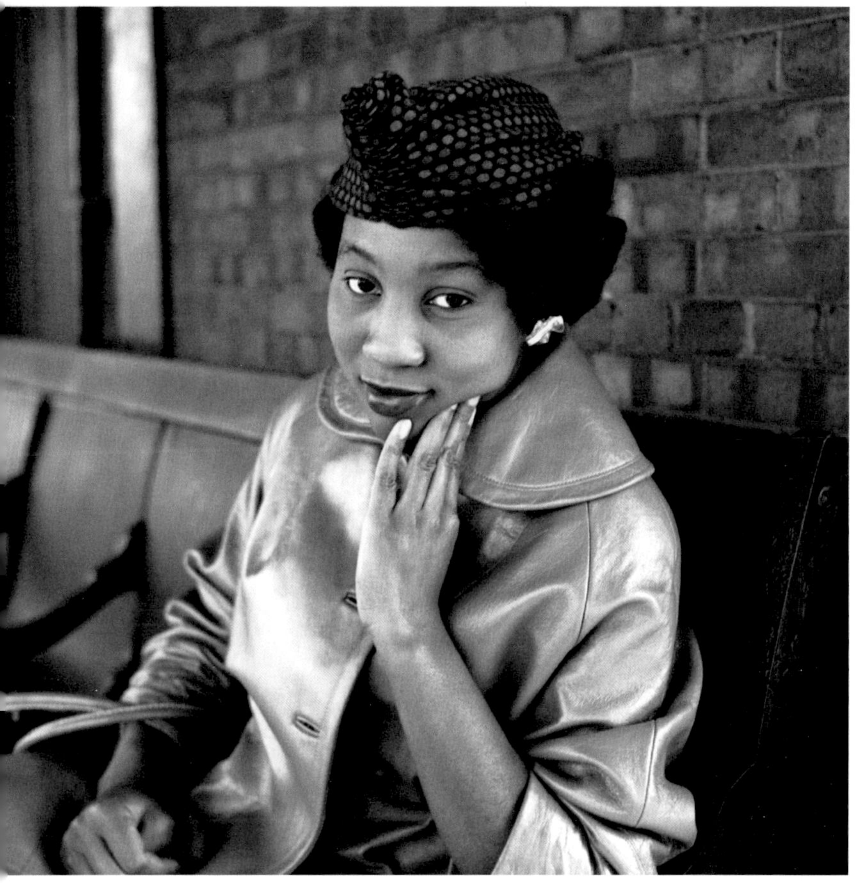

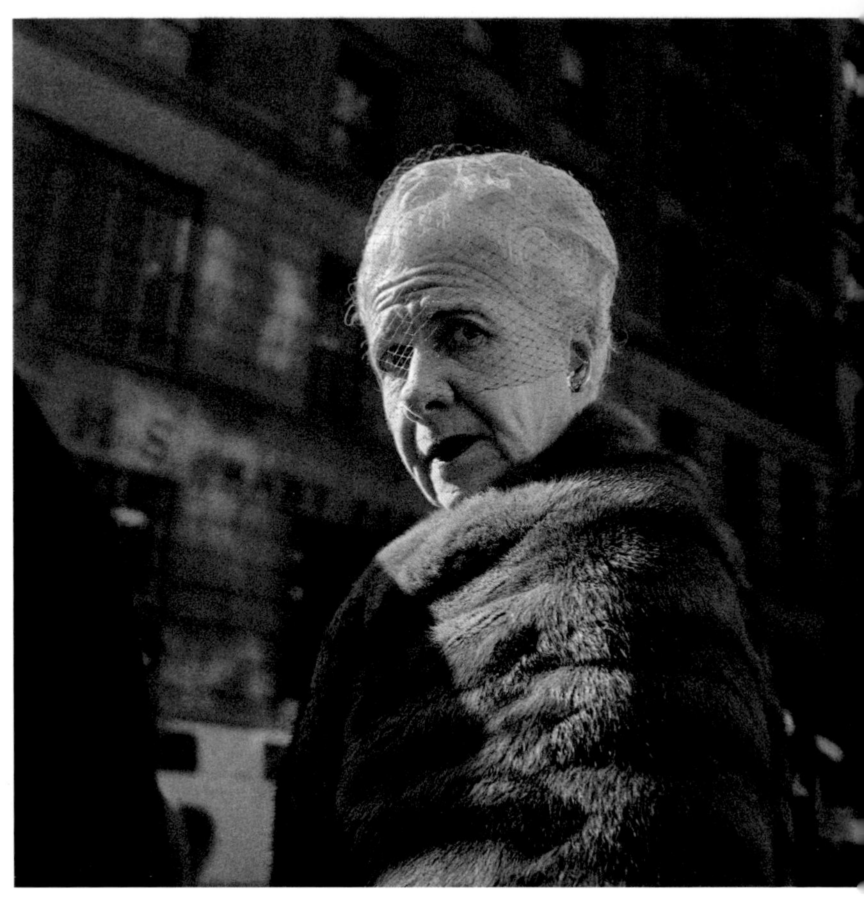

25. New York, January 26, 1955.

26. New York, September 1959.

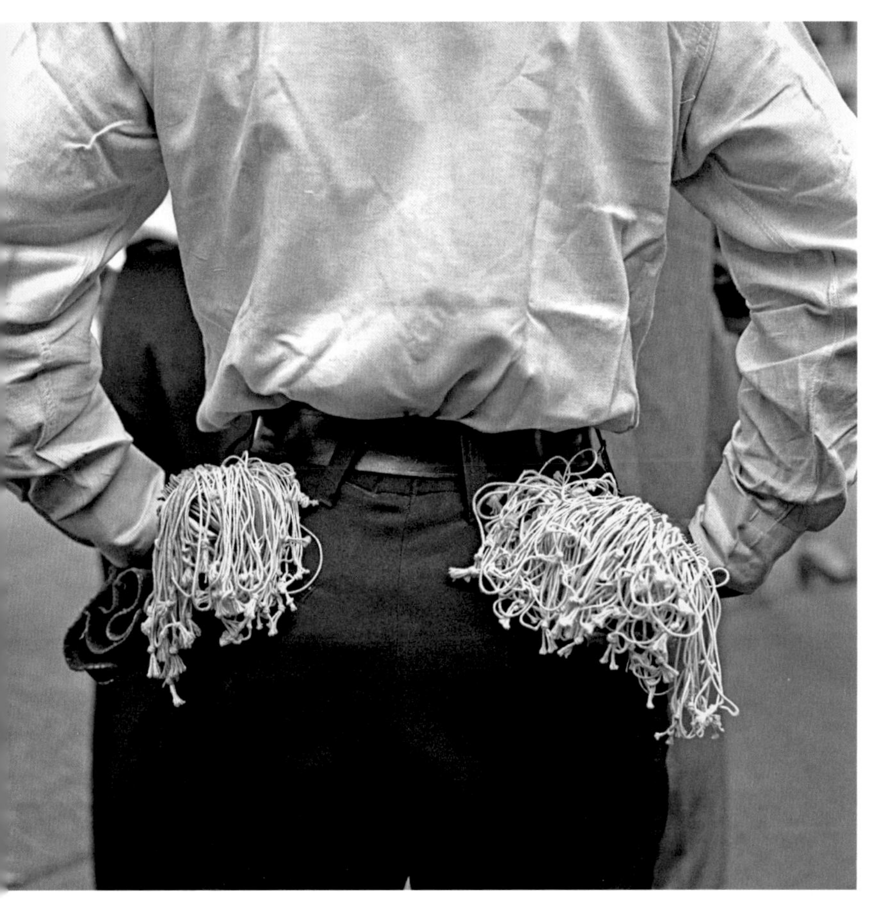

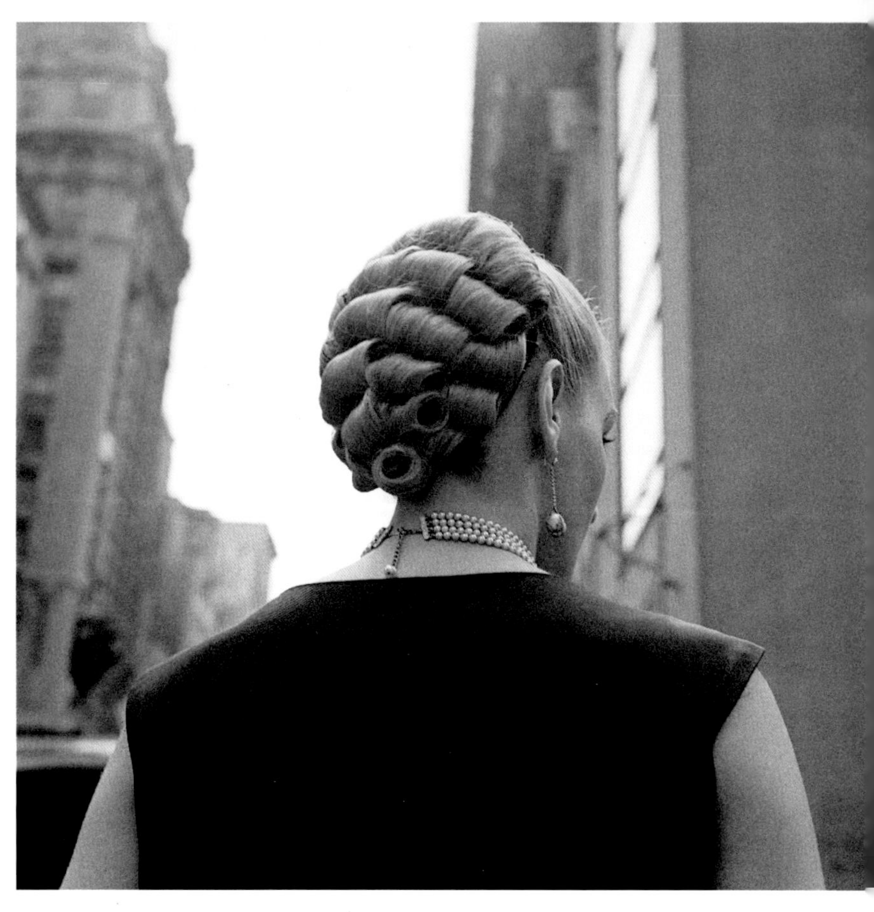

27. New York, September 3, 1954.
28. New York, September 1956.

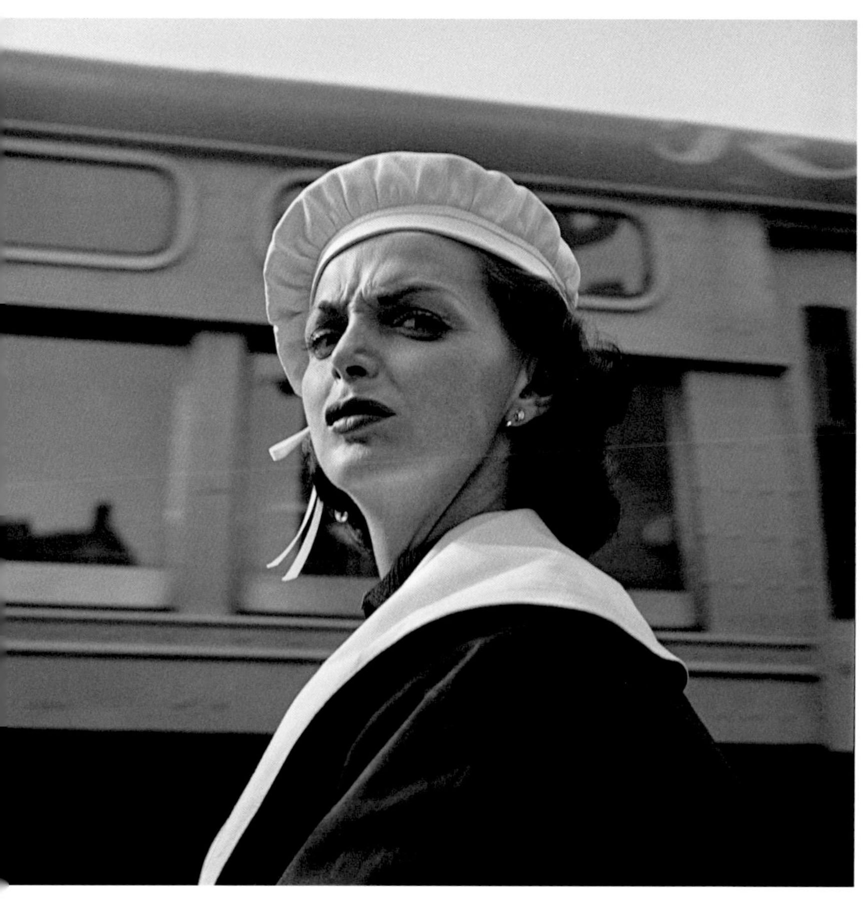

29. New York, September 29, 1959.

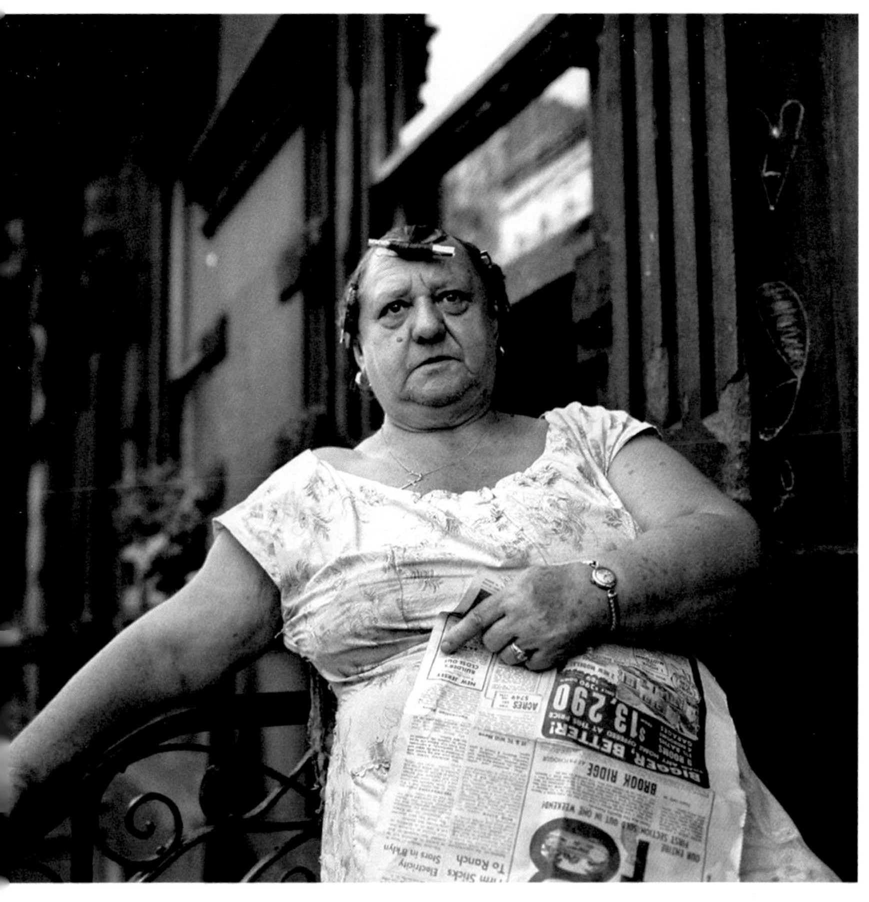

BROOK RIDGE
BIGGER, BETTER!
$13,290
ACRES
NEW JERSEY
Firm Sticks Electricity
To Ranch
Stars In B'klyn

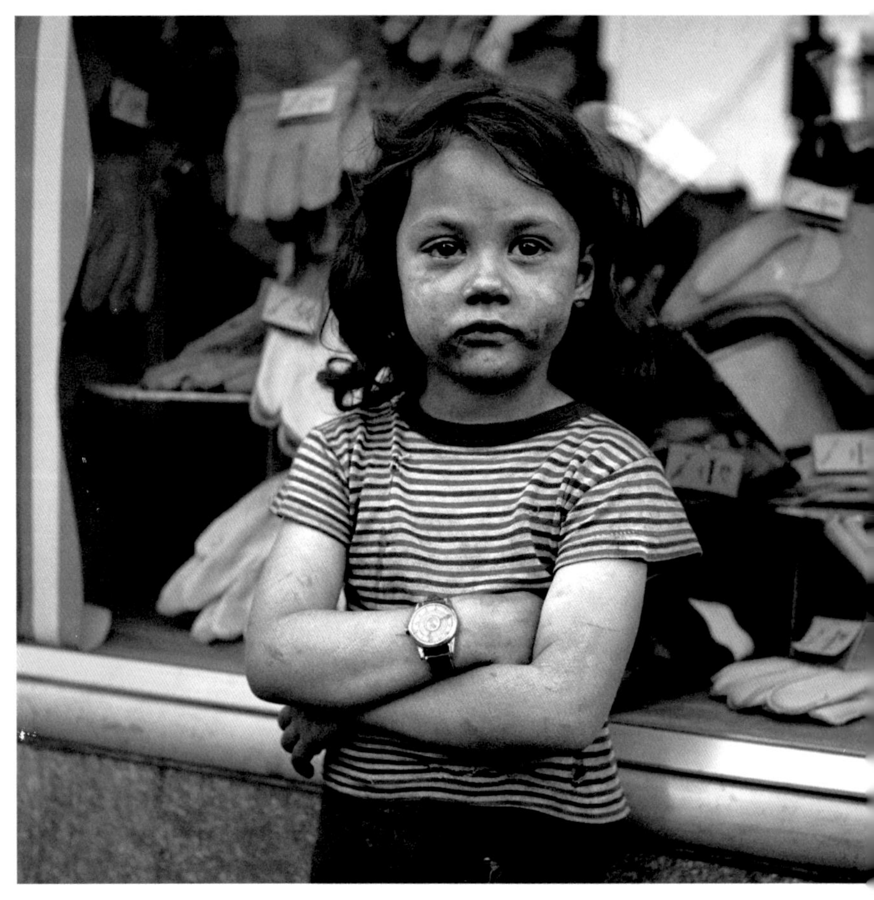

30. Canada, 1955.

31. New York Public Library, ca. 1954.

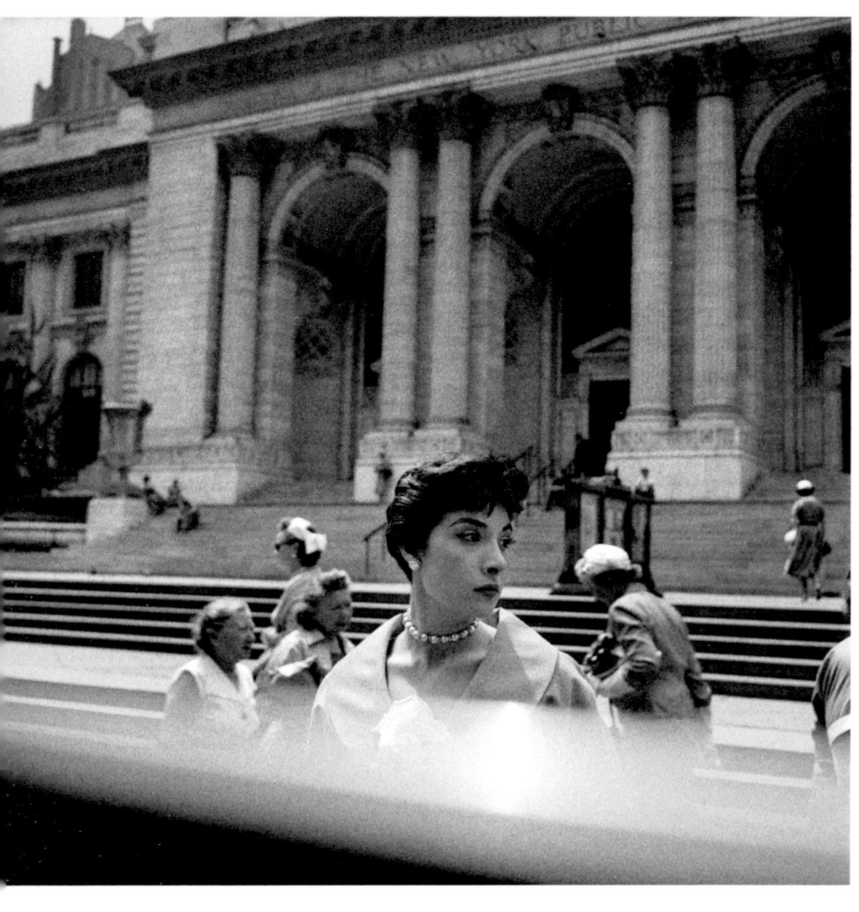

32. New York, March 1954.

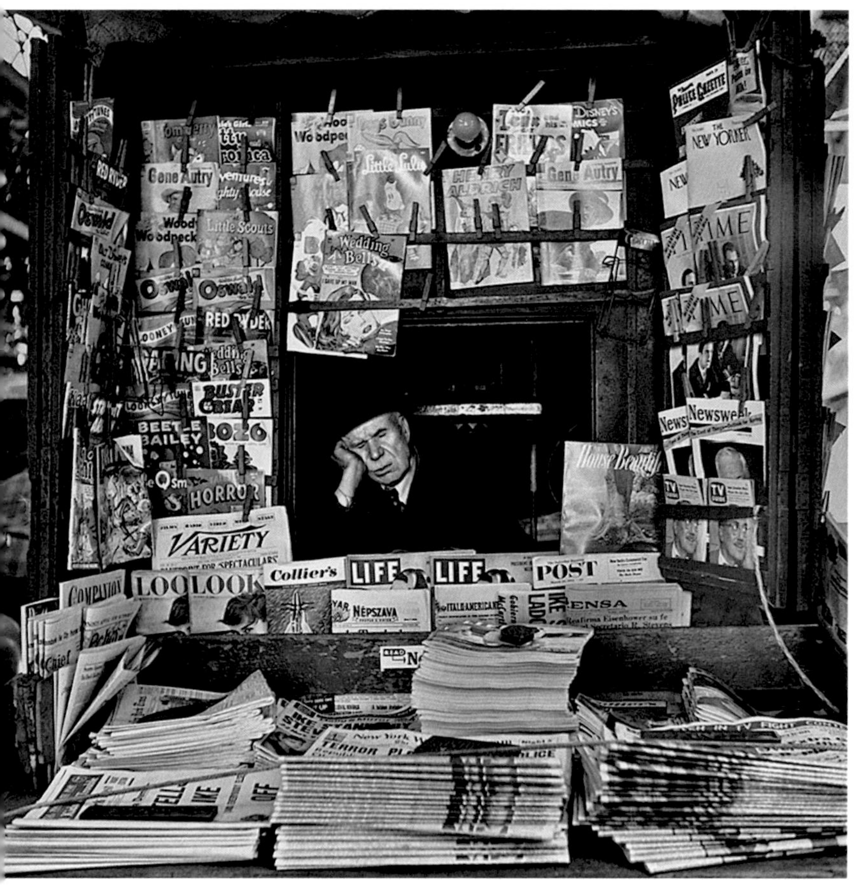

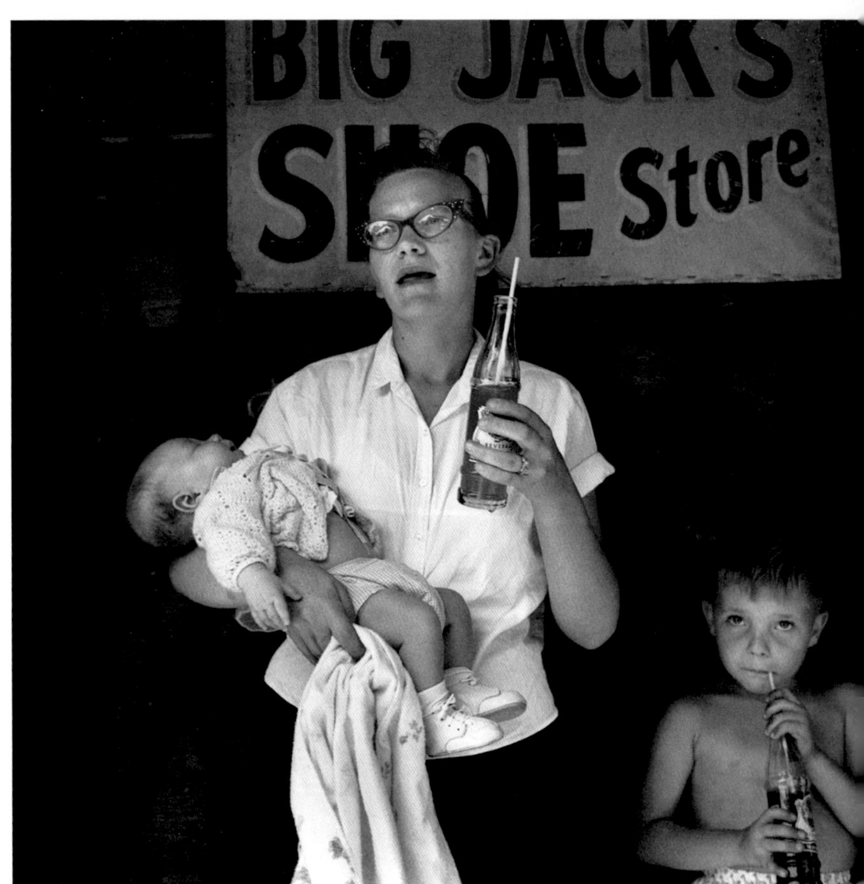

33. Chicago, 1962.
34. Grenoble, 1959.

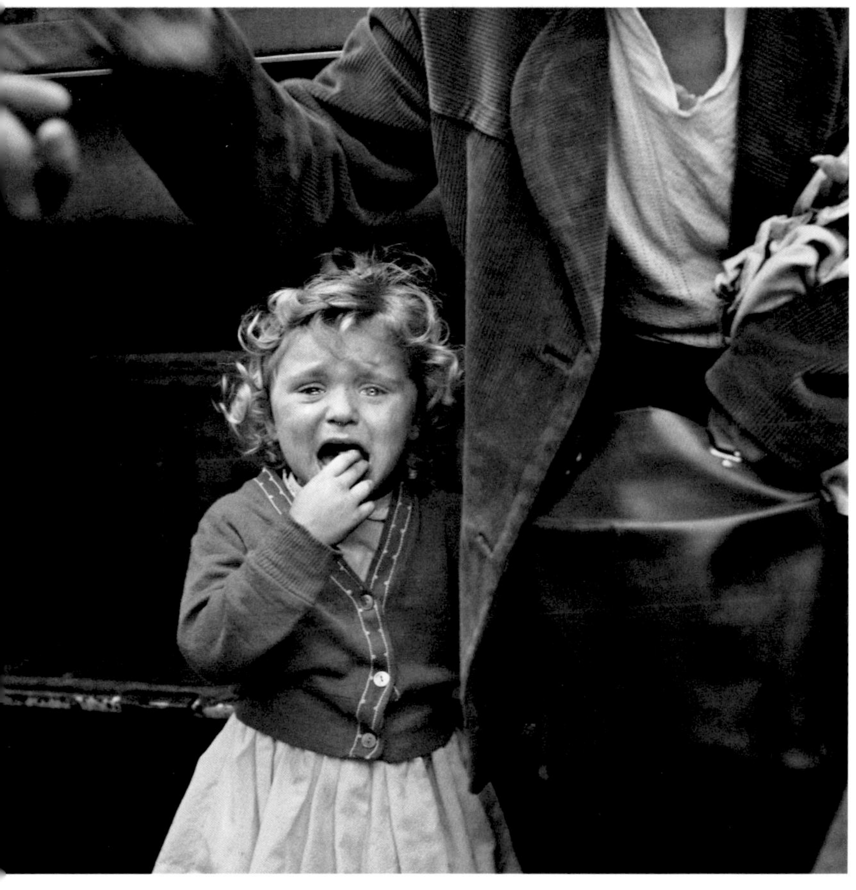

35. Chicago, 1962.

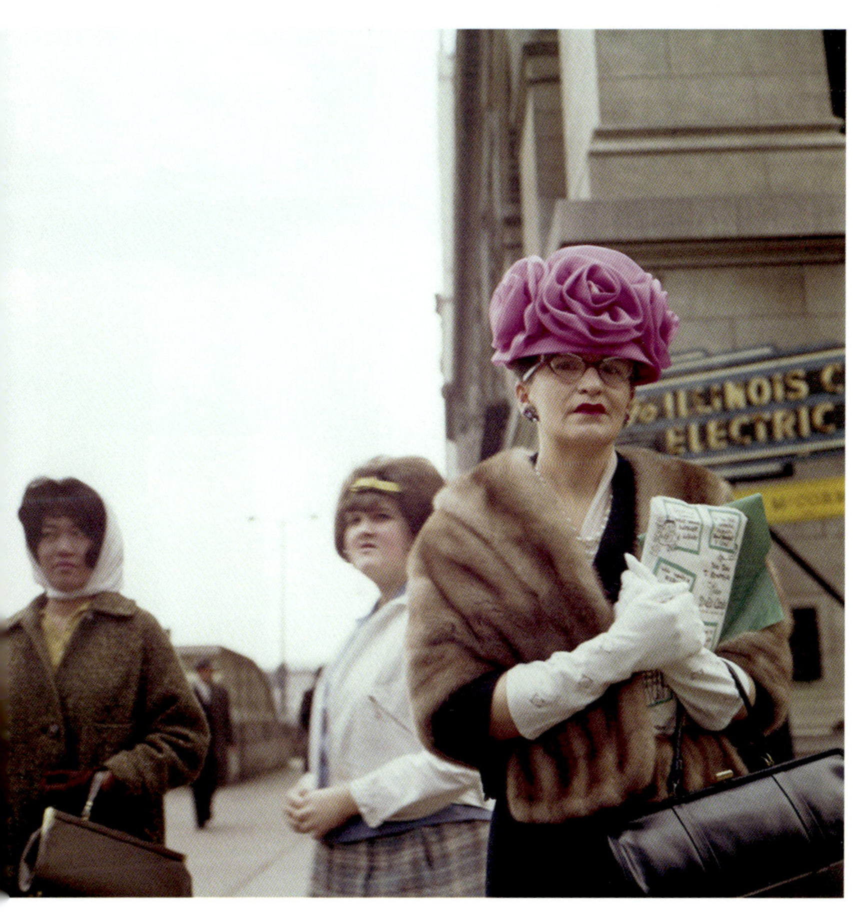
ILLINOIS
ELECTRIC

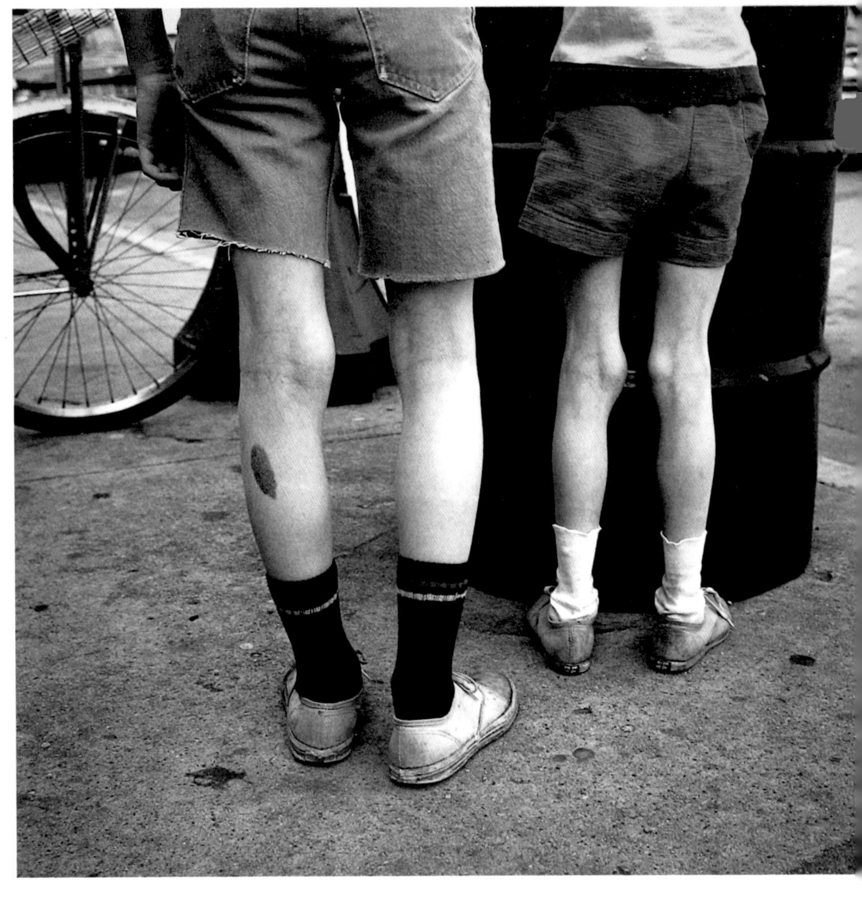

36. Chicago, early 1970s.

37. Self-portrait, Chicago.

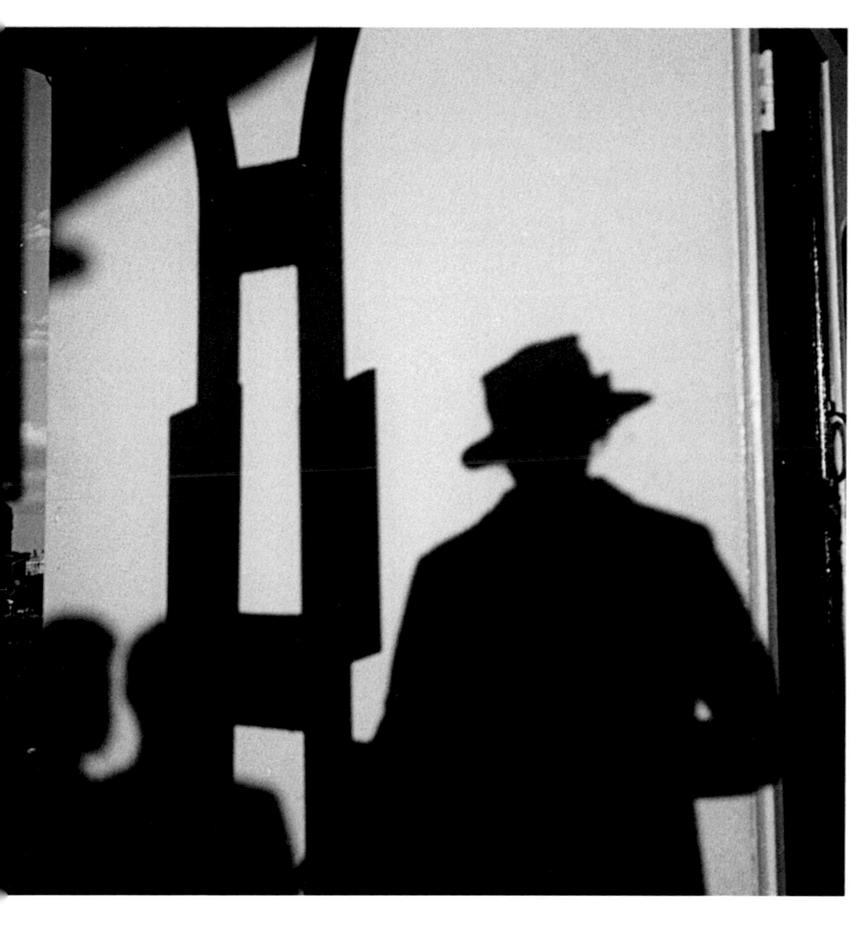

38. Chicago, June 1978.

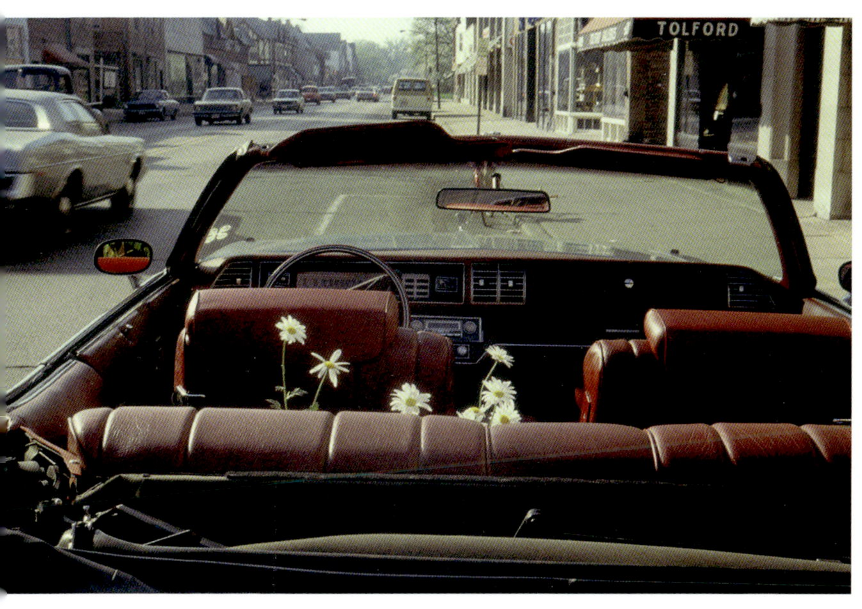

TOLFORD

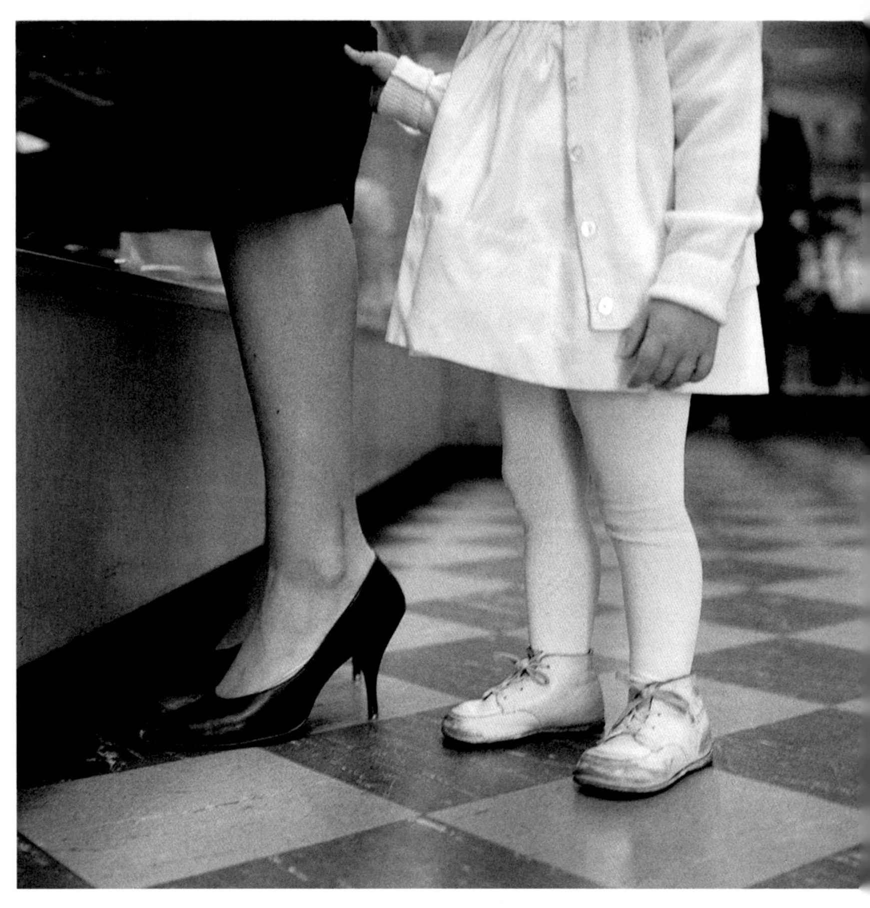

39. September 18, 1962.

40. Chicago, 1956.

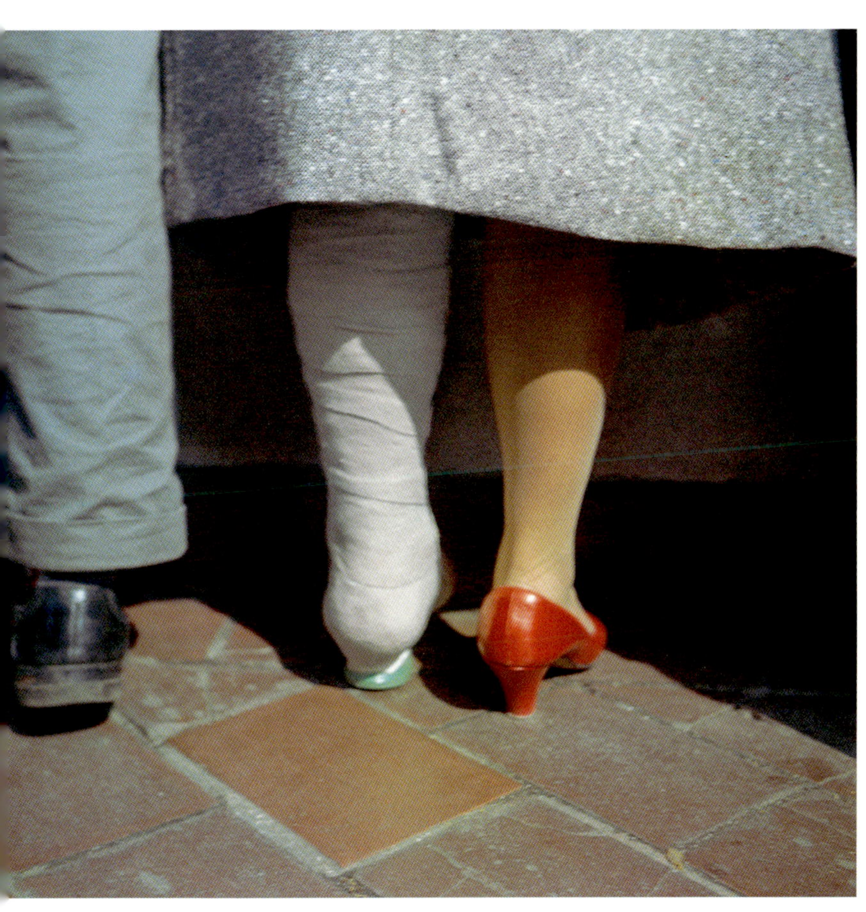

41. Chicago.

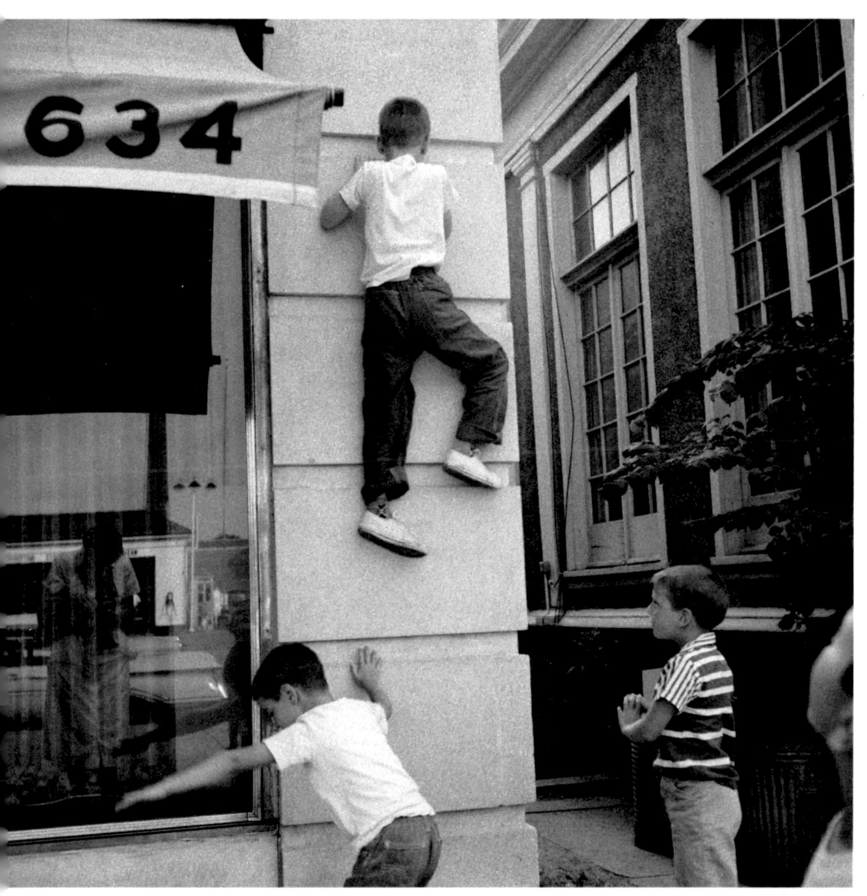

634

42. New York, October 10, 1954.

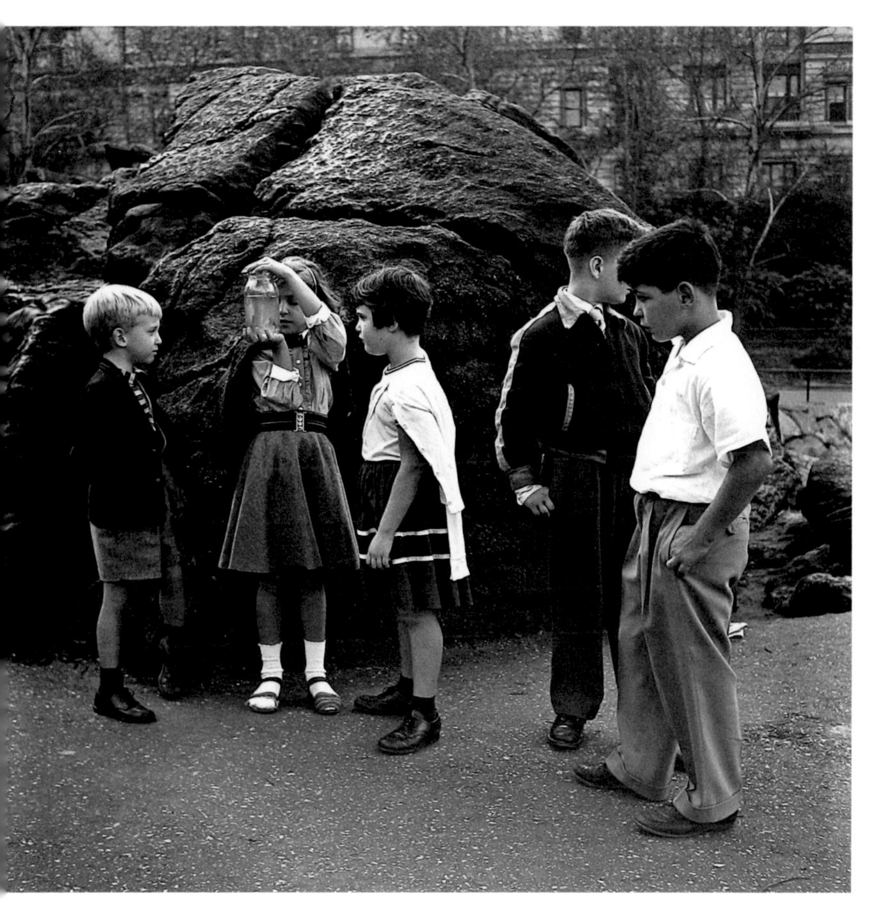

43. New York, 1953.

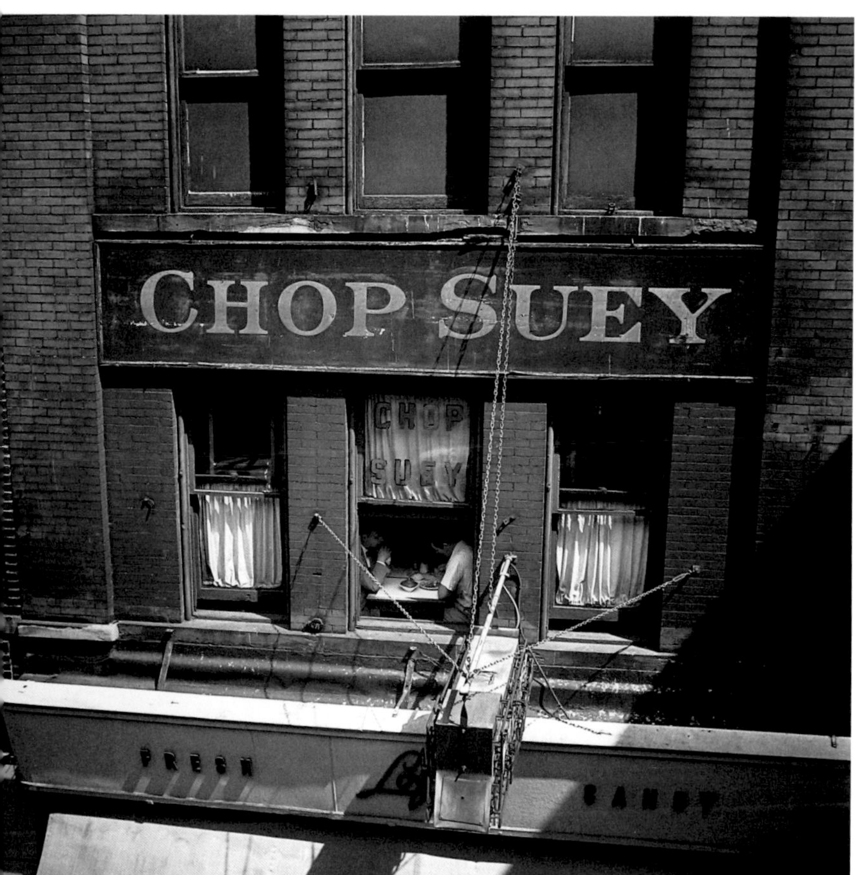
CHOP SUEY
CHOP
SUEY
FRESH
CANDY

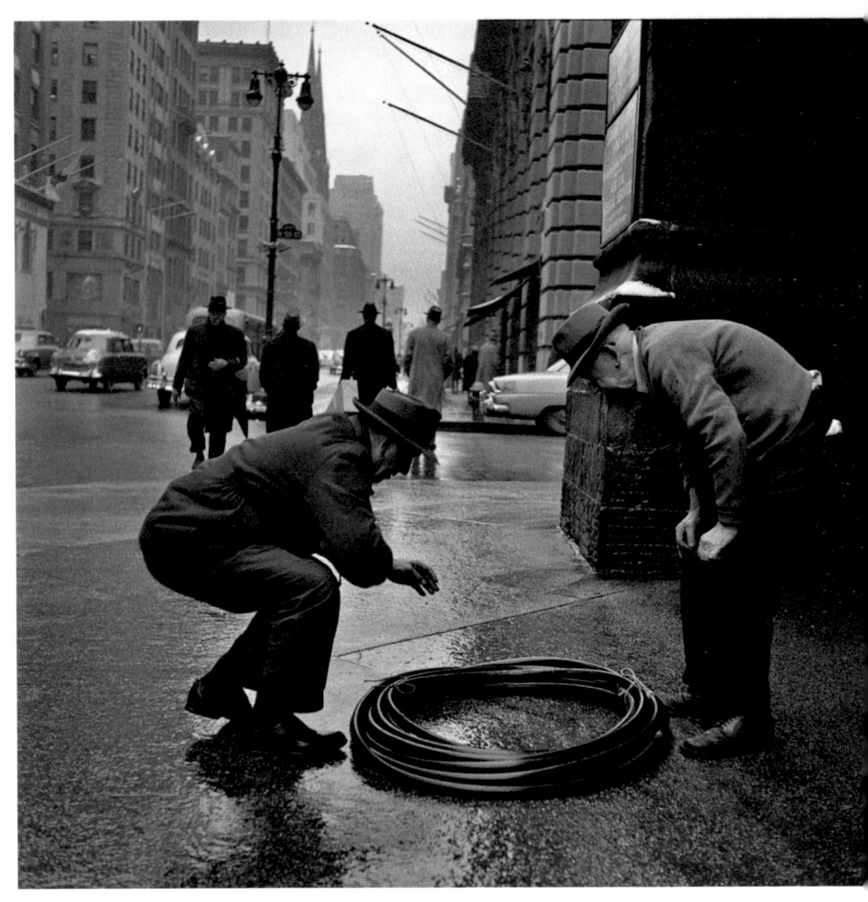

44. New York, 1953.

45. Armenian woman, East 86th Street, New York, September 1956.

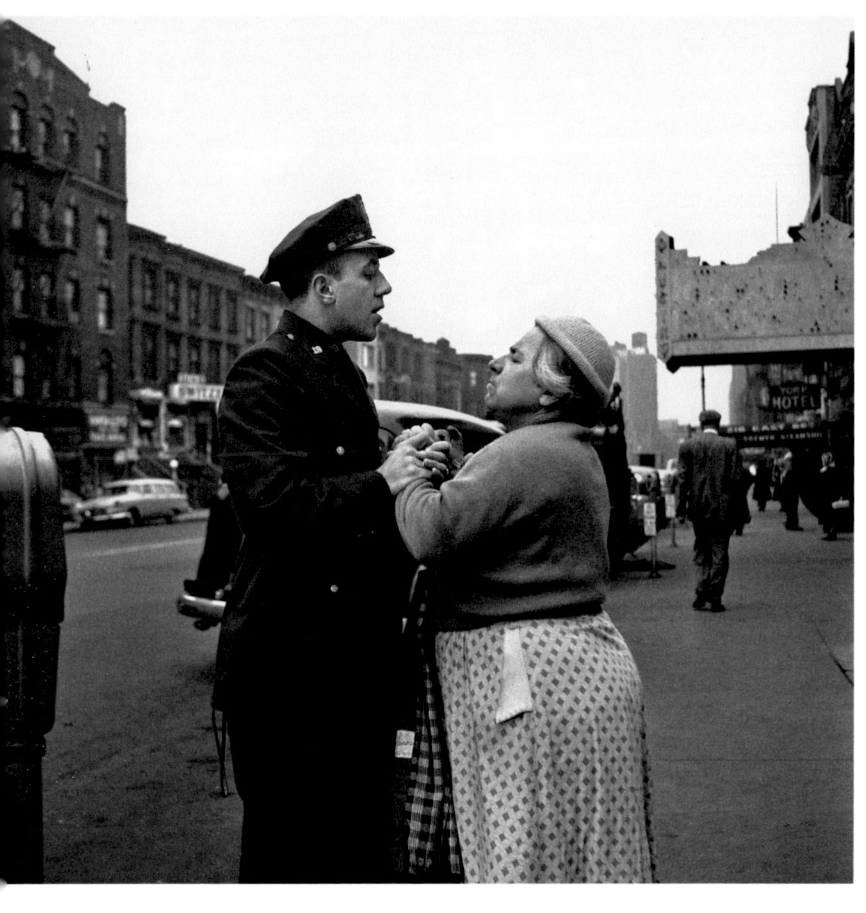

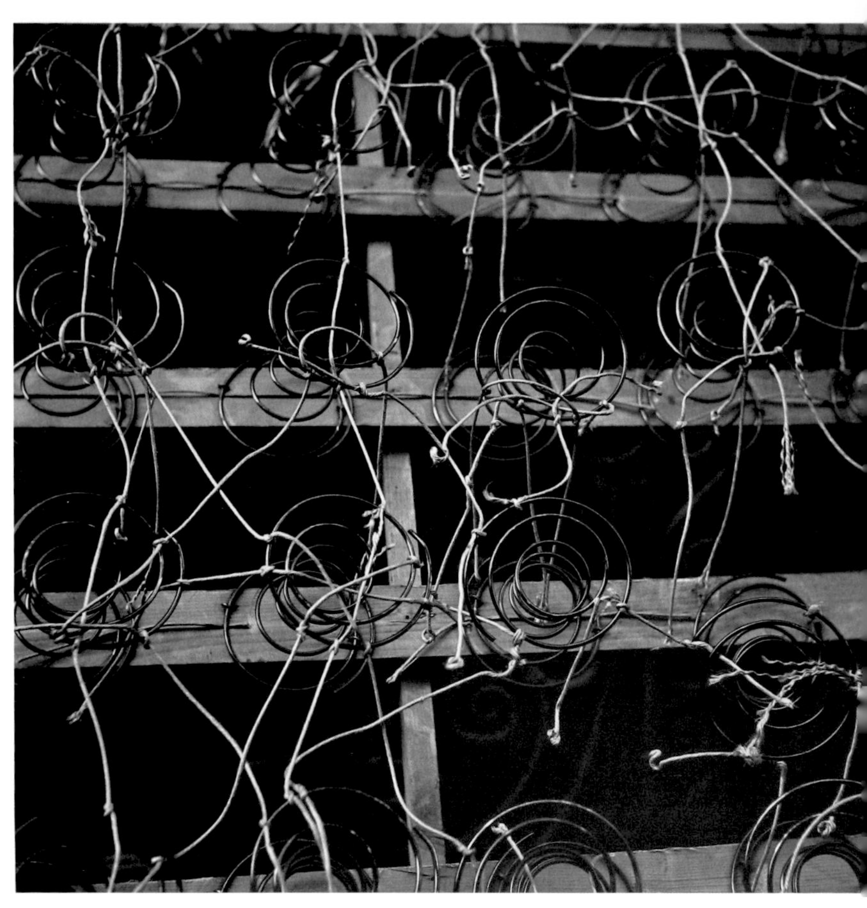

46. Location and date unknown.

47. New York, 1955.

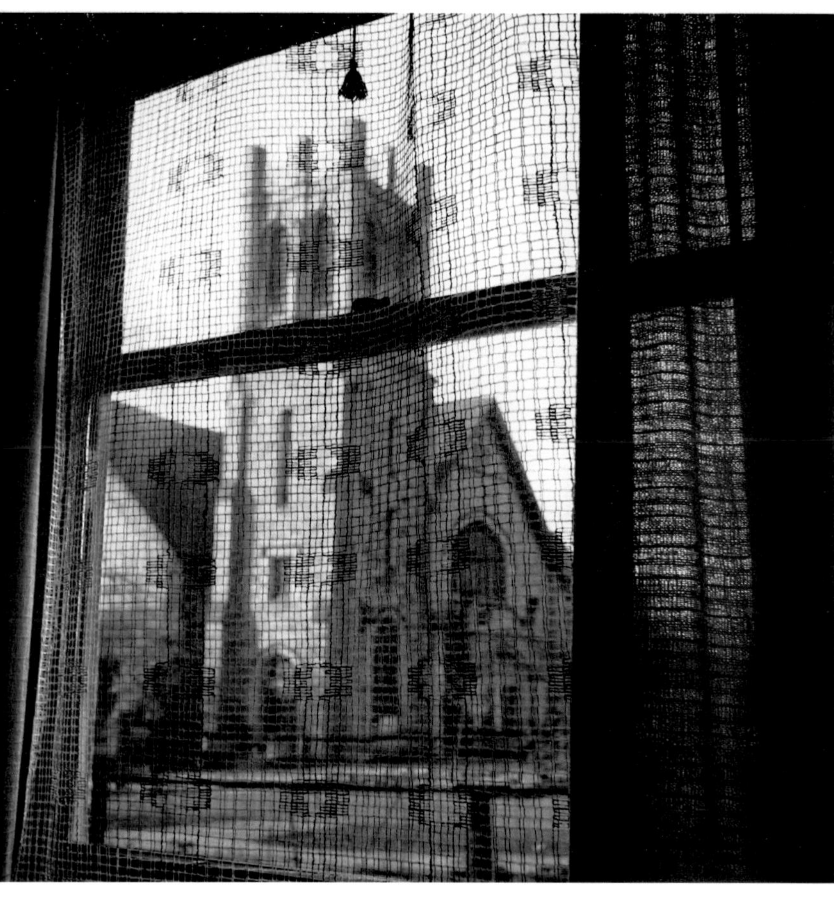

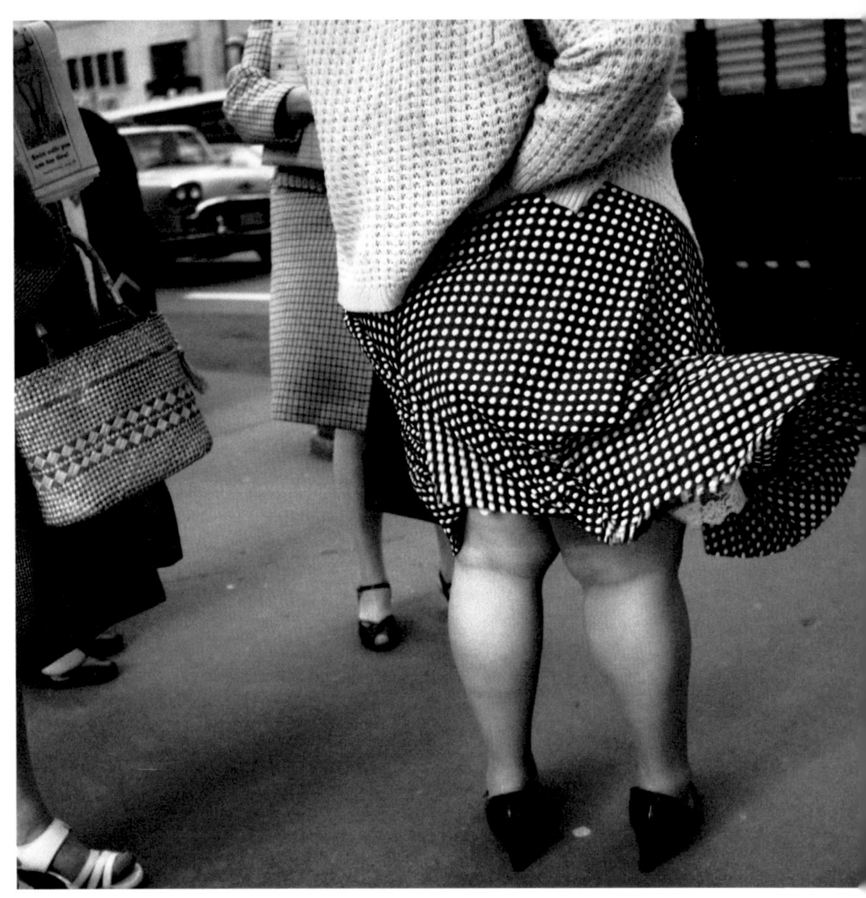

48. Chicago, May 27, 1970.
49. Location and date unknown.

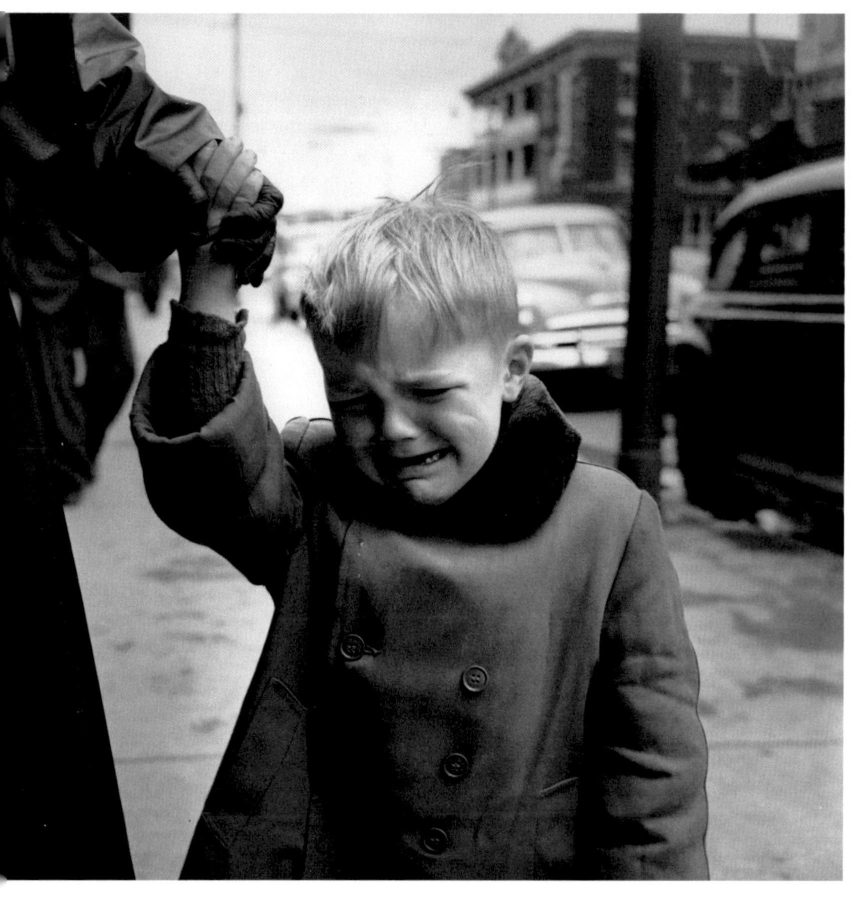

50. Self-portrait, Chicago, 1970.

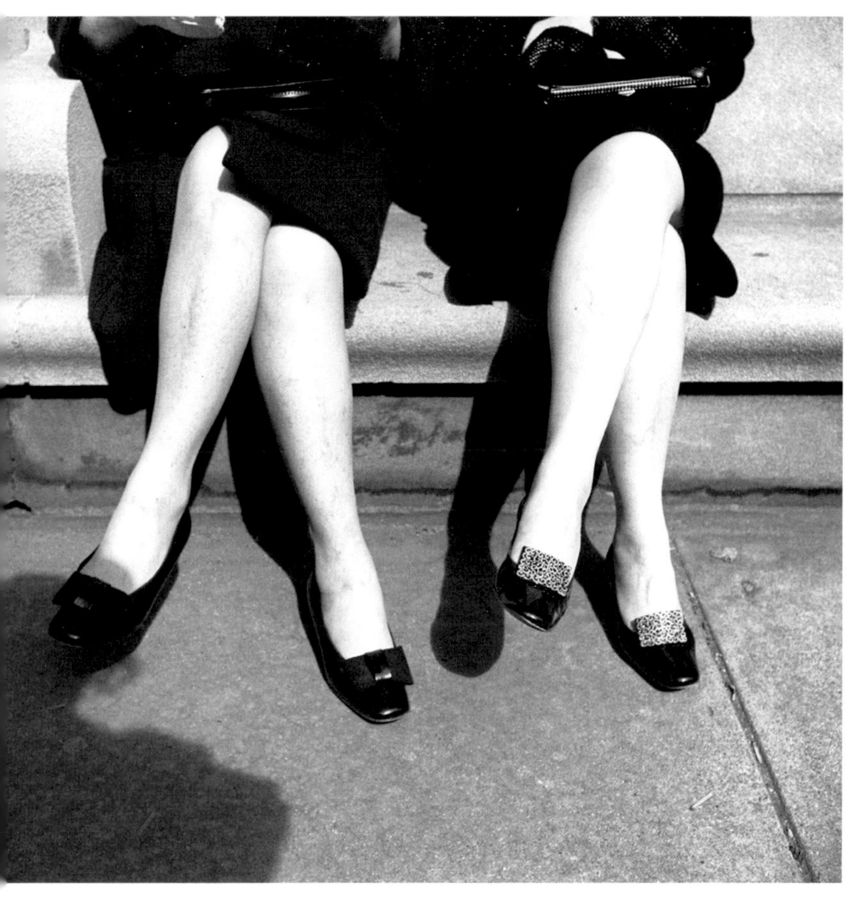

51. New York, 1954.

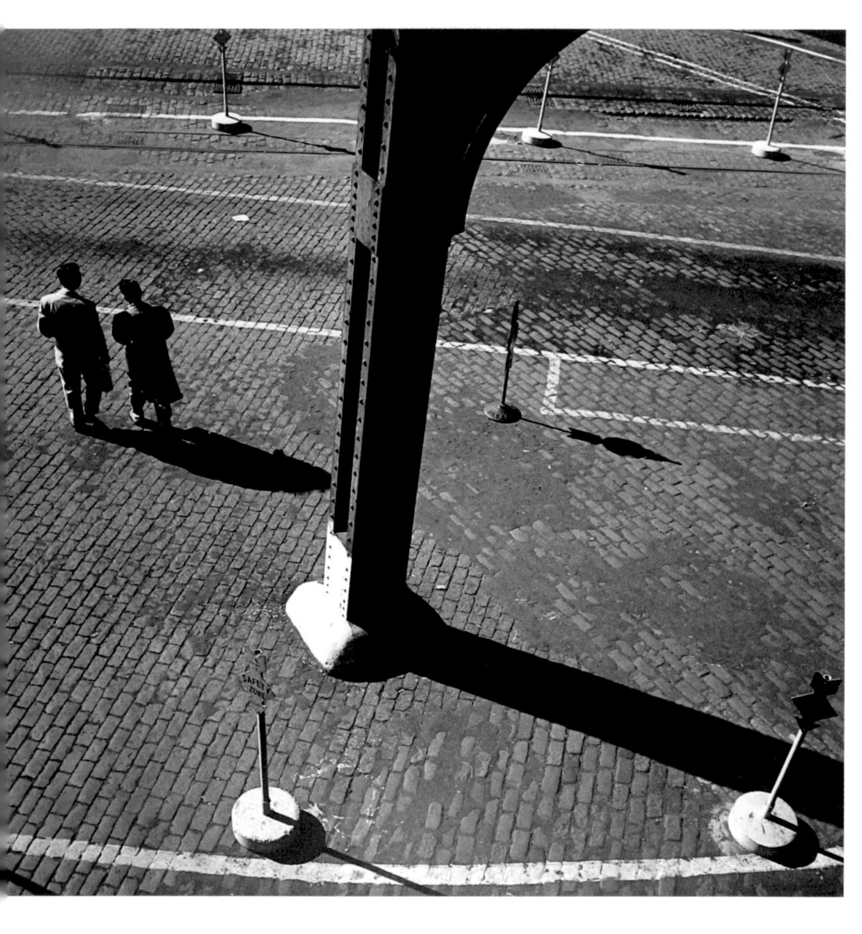

52. Florida, January 9, 1957.

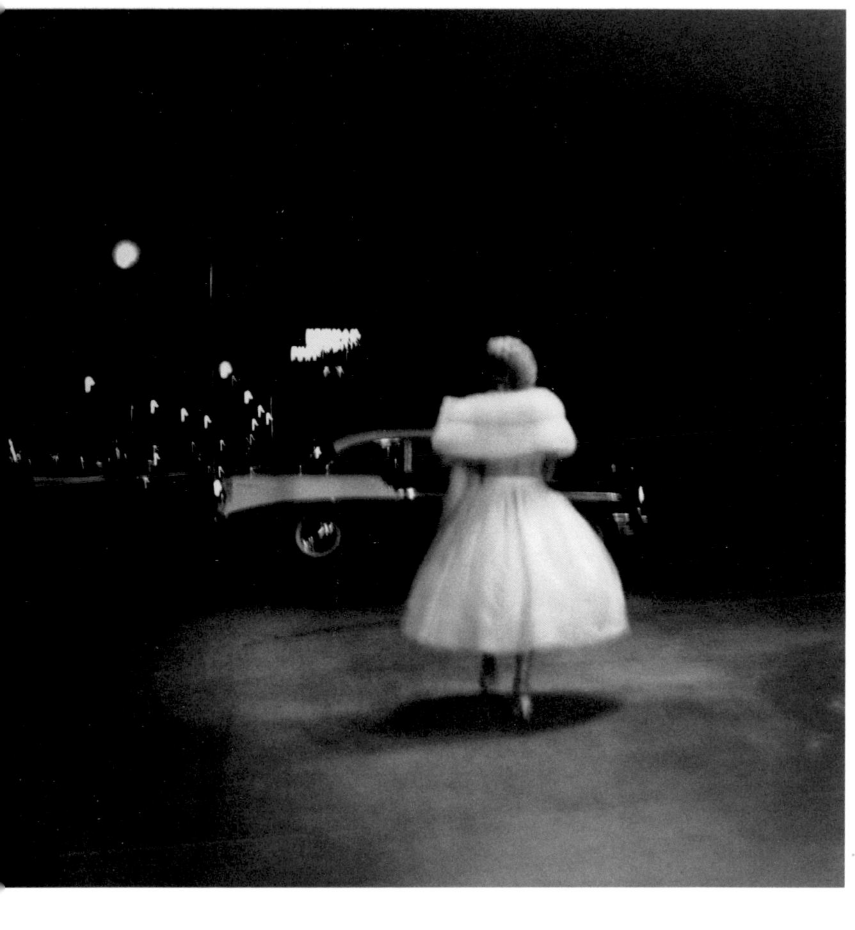

53. May 1979.

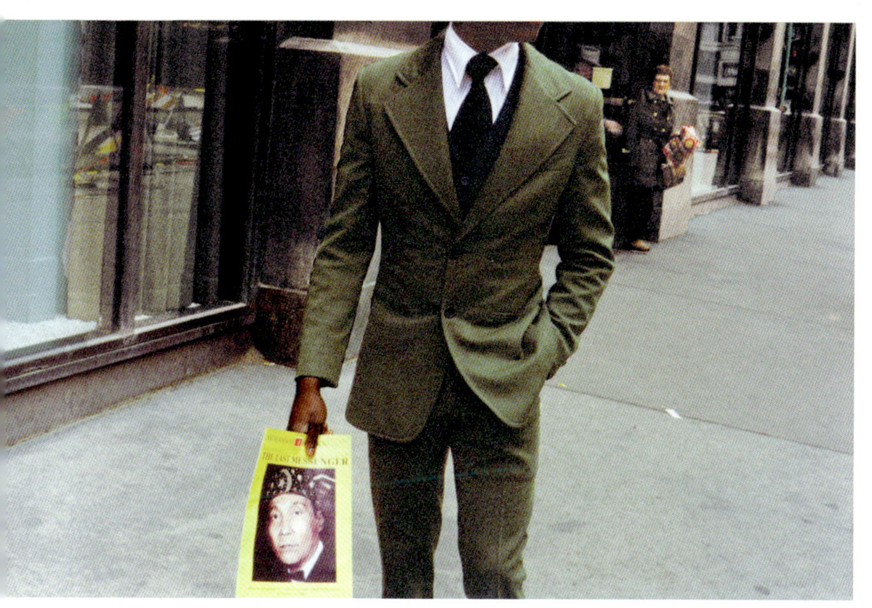

THE LAST MESSENGER

54. New York, 1954.

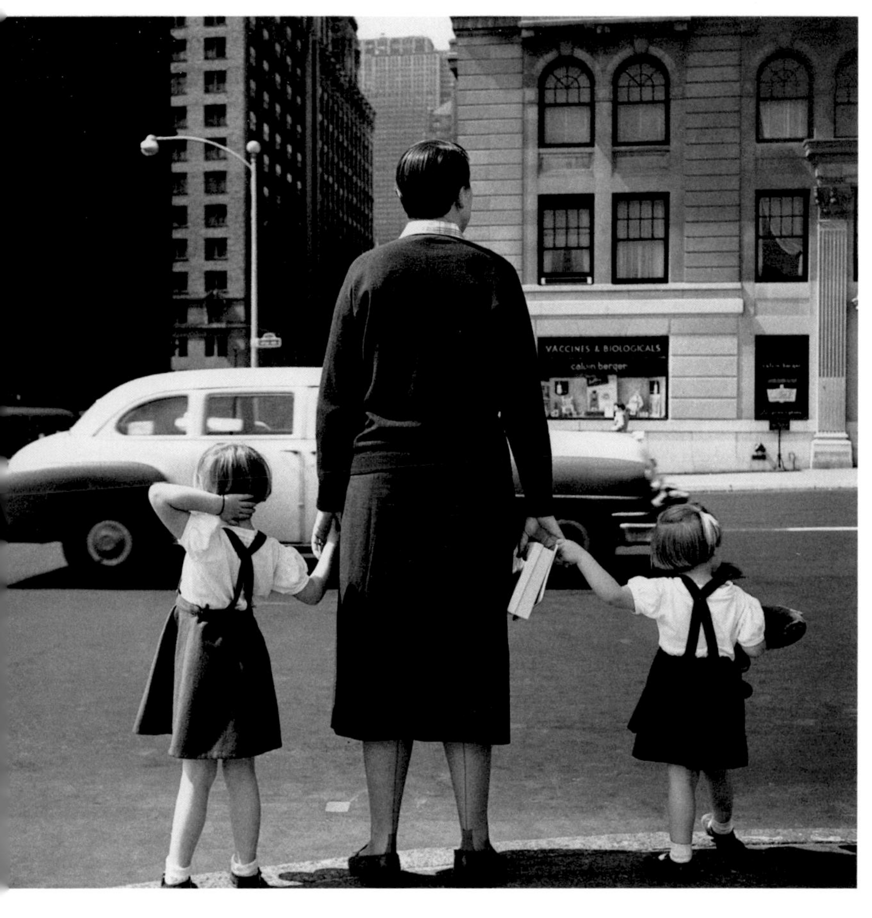

VACCINES & BIOLOGICALS
calvin berger

55. August 1975.

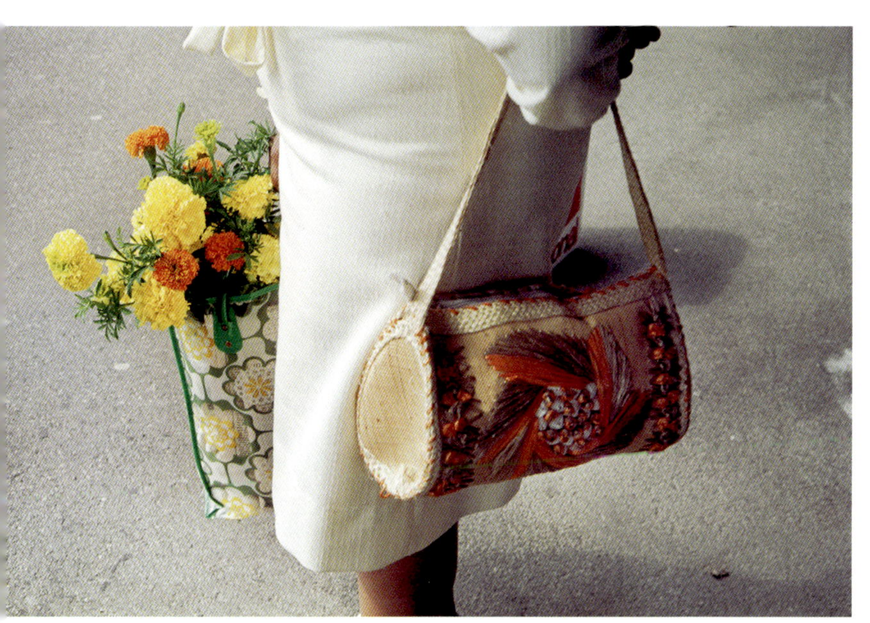

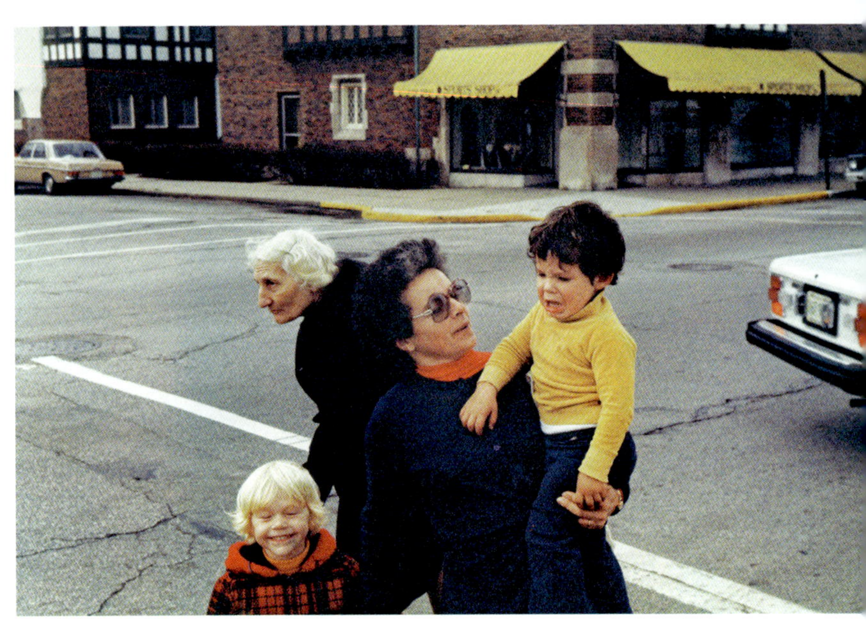

56. Chicago, 1977.

57. Self-portrait, 1954.

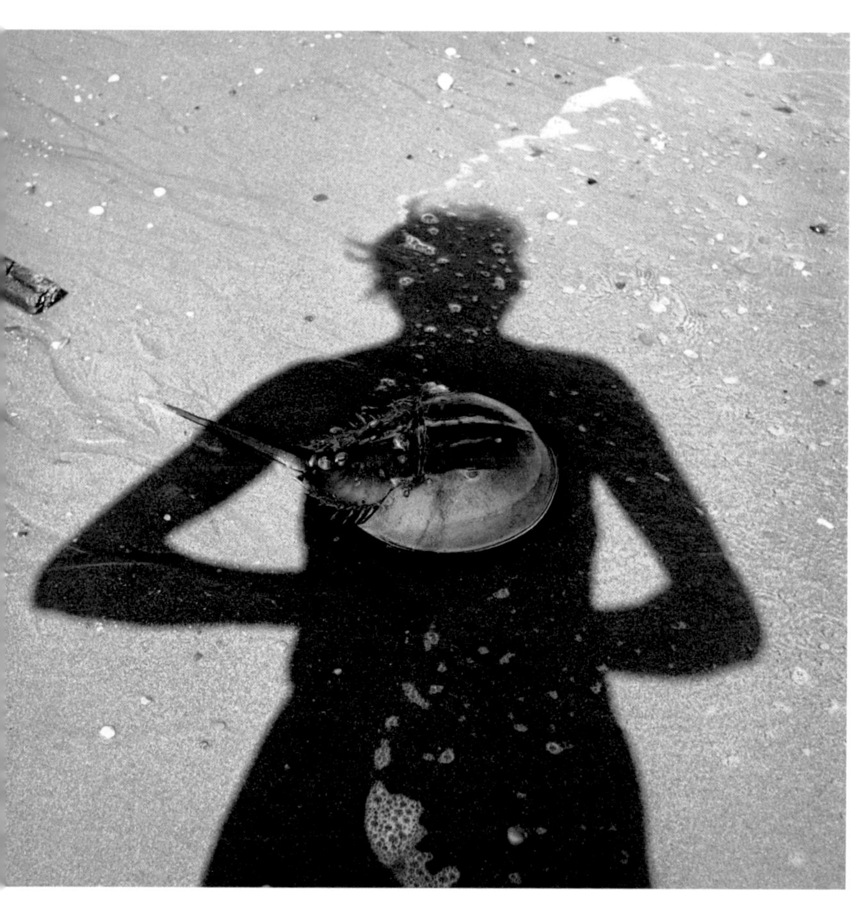

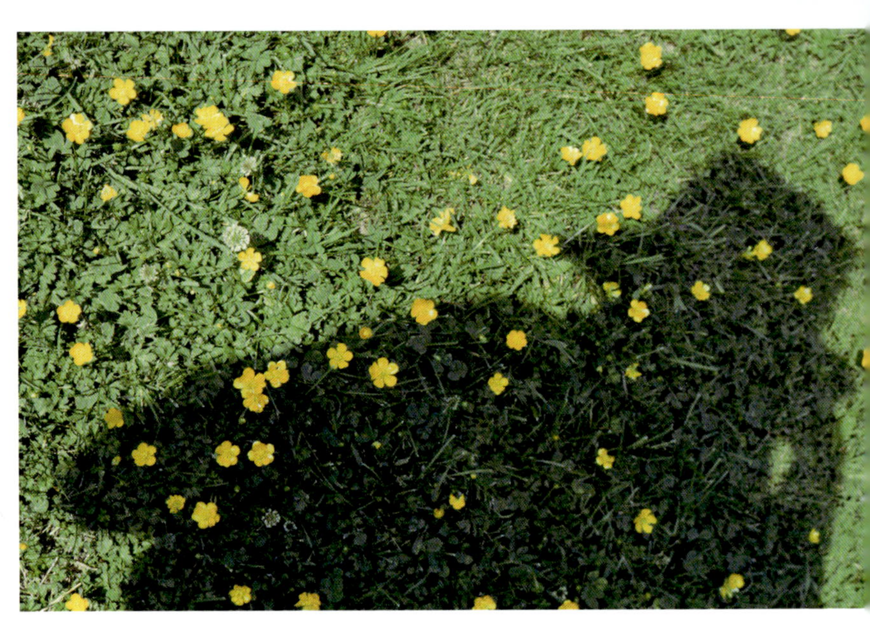

58. Self-portrait, 1975.
59. Self-portrait, Chicago.

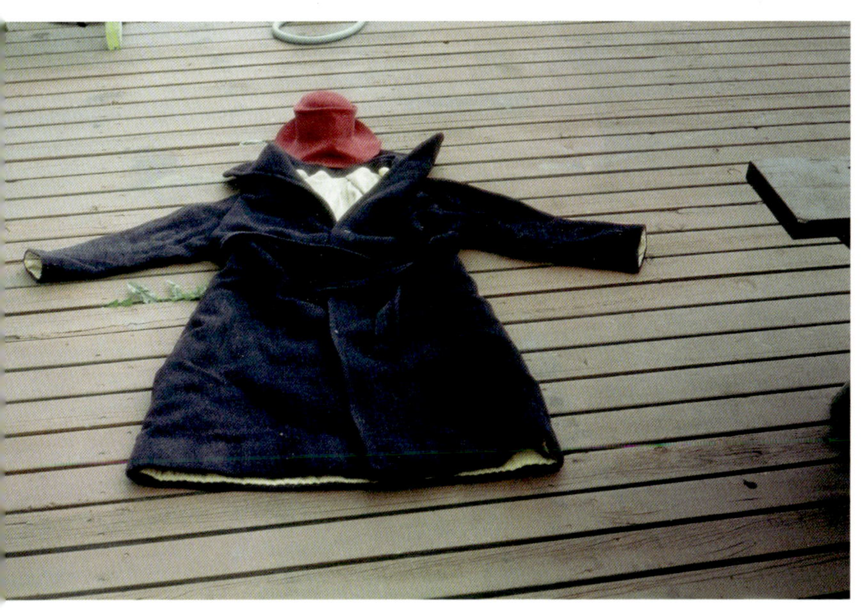

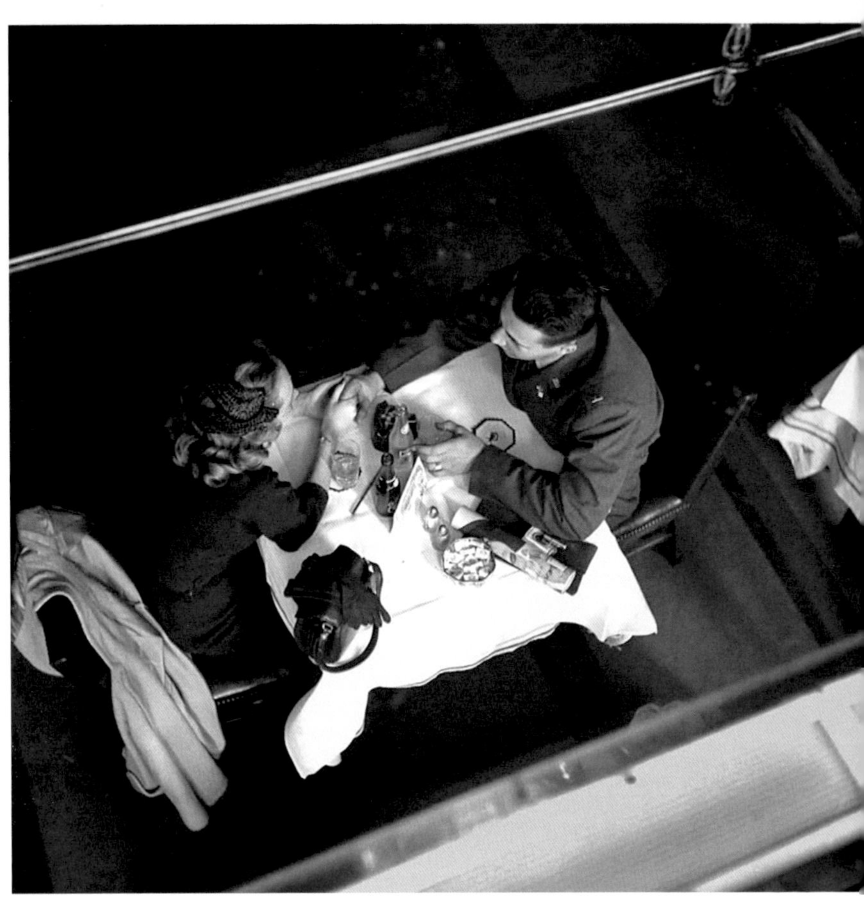

60. New York, April 1953.

61. Self-portrait, Chicago, July 27, 1971.

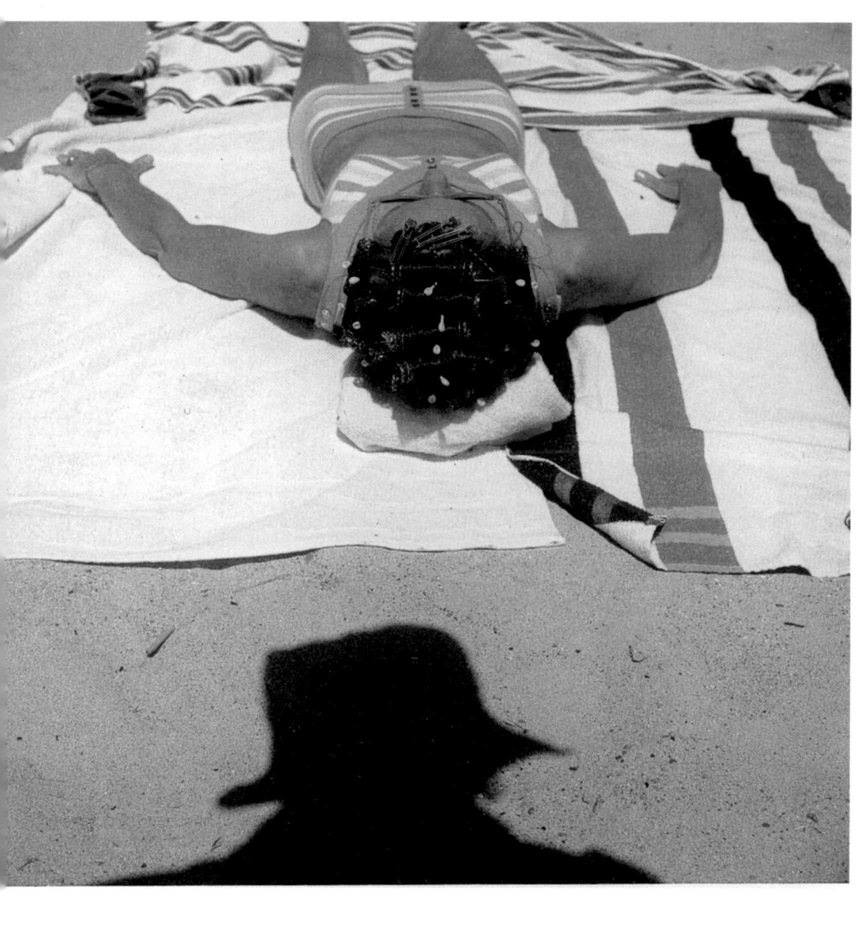

62. Chicago, 1958.

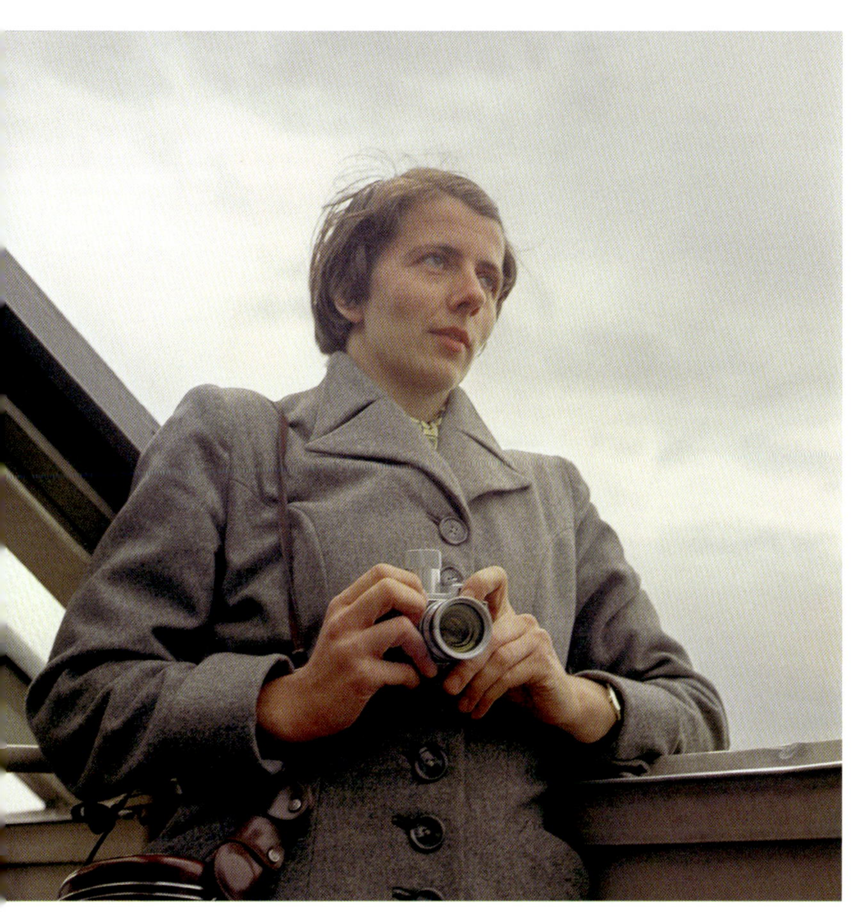

63. New York, September 1953.

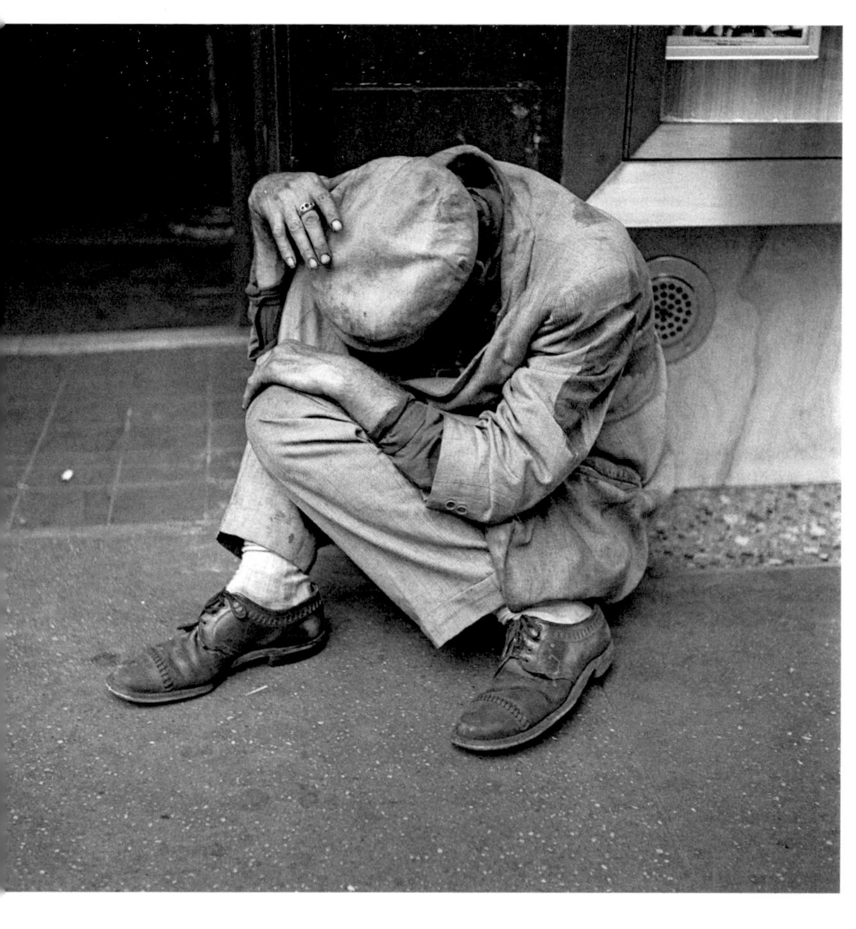

64. Self-portrait, May 5, 1955.

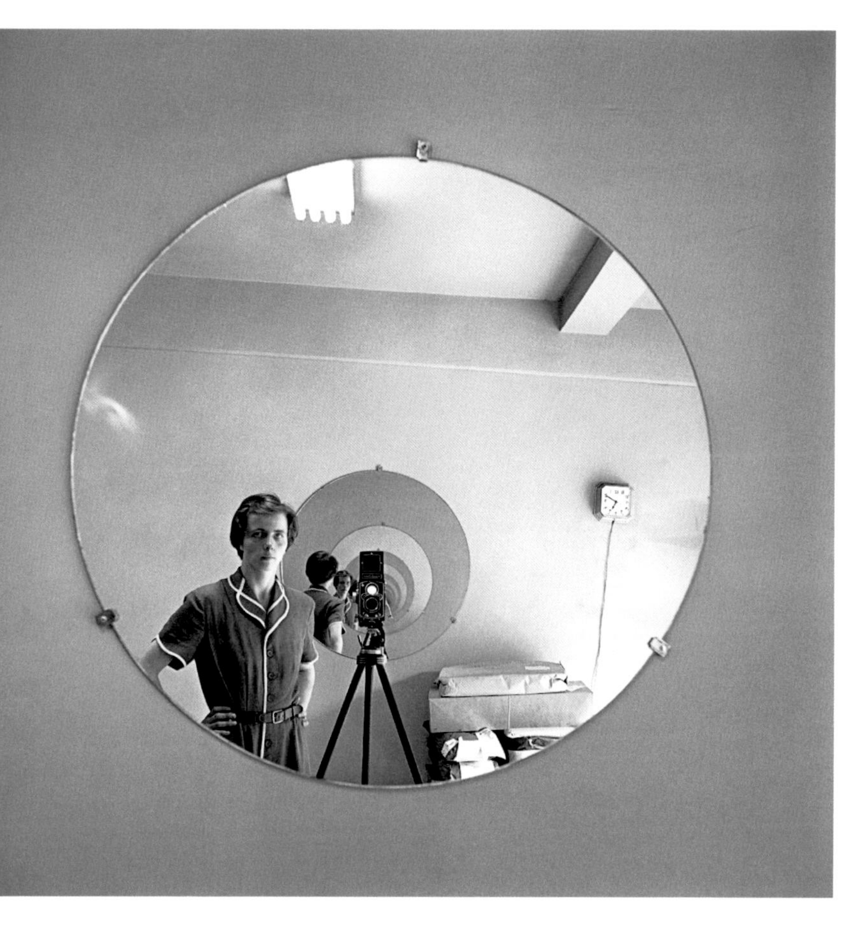

65. Chicago, June 16, 1956.

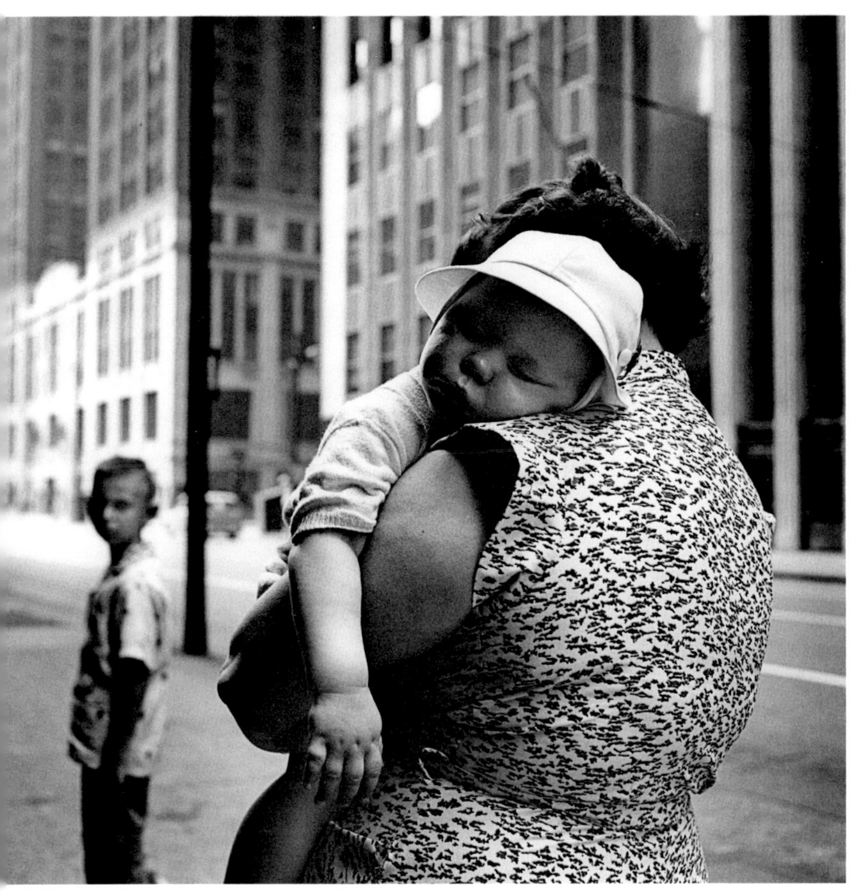

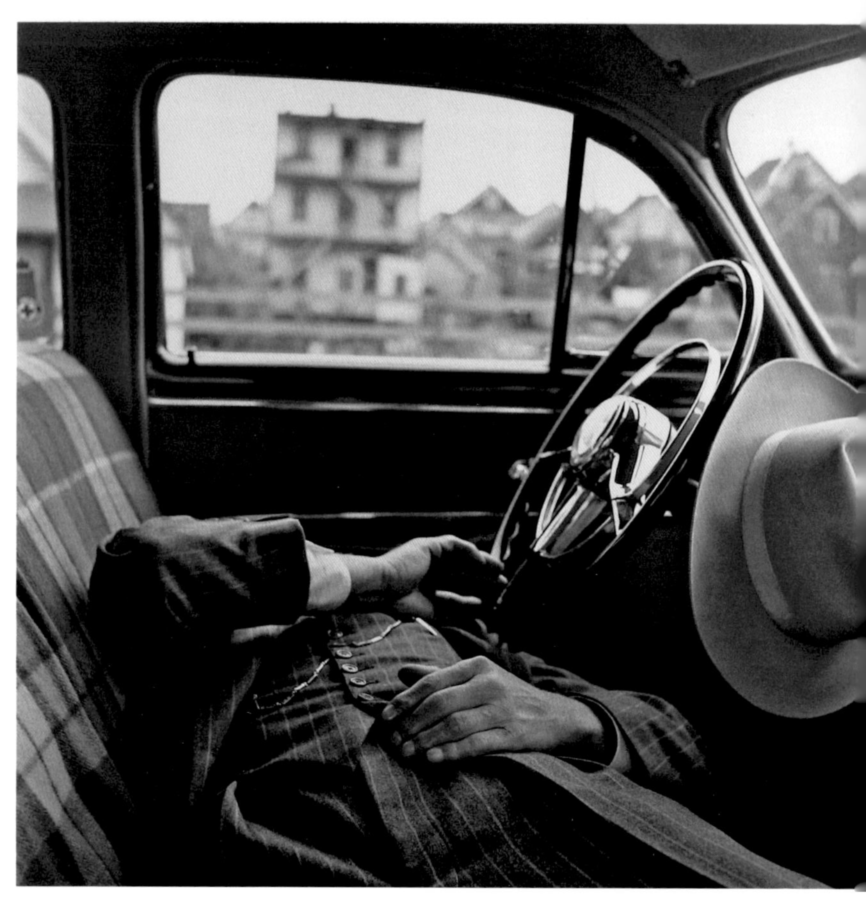

66. New York, ca. 1953.
67. New York, 1954.

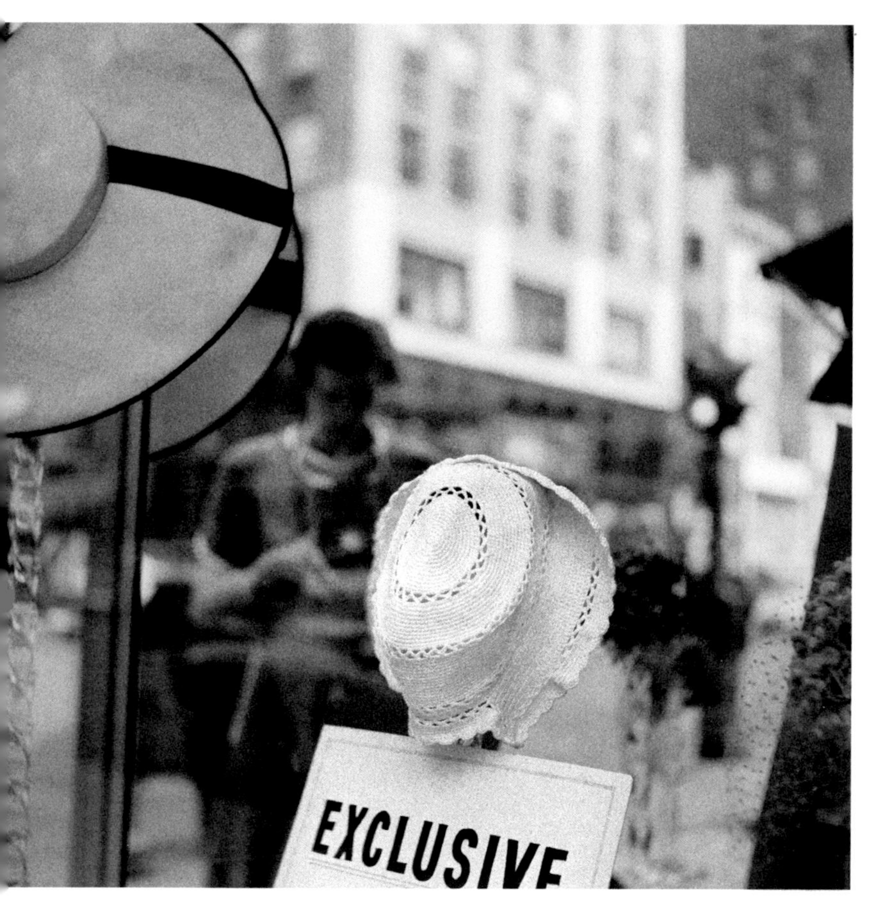
EXCLUSIVE

68. Self-portrait.

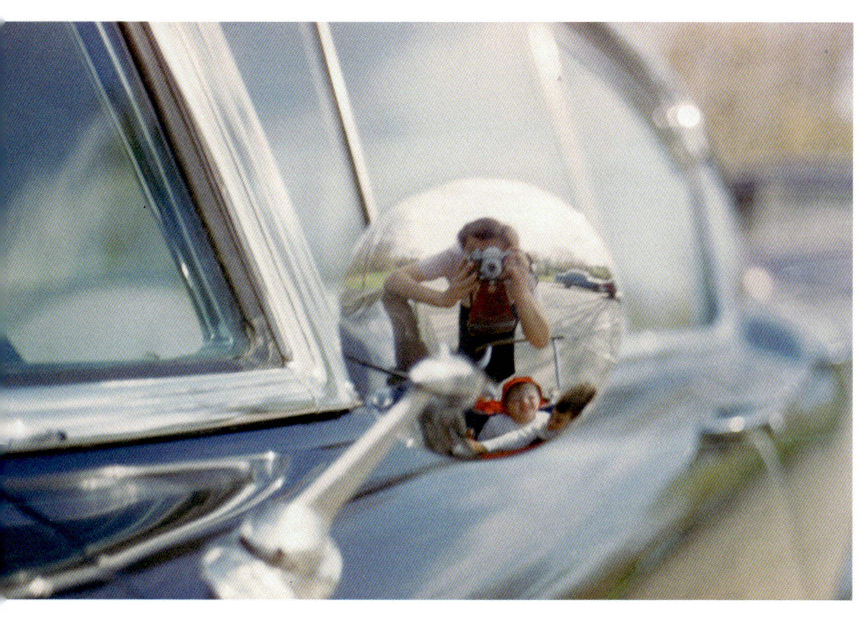

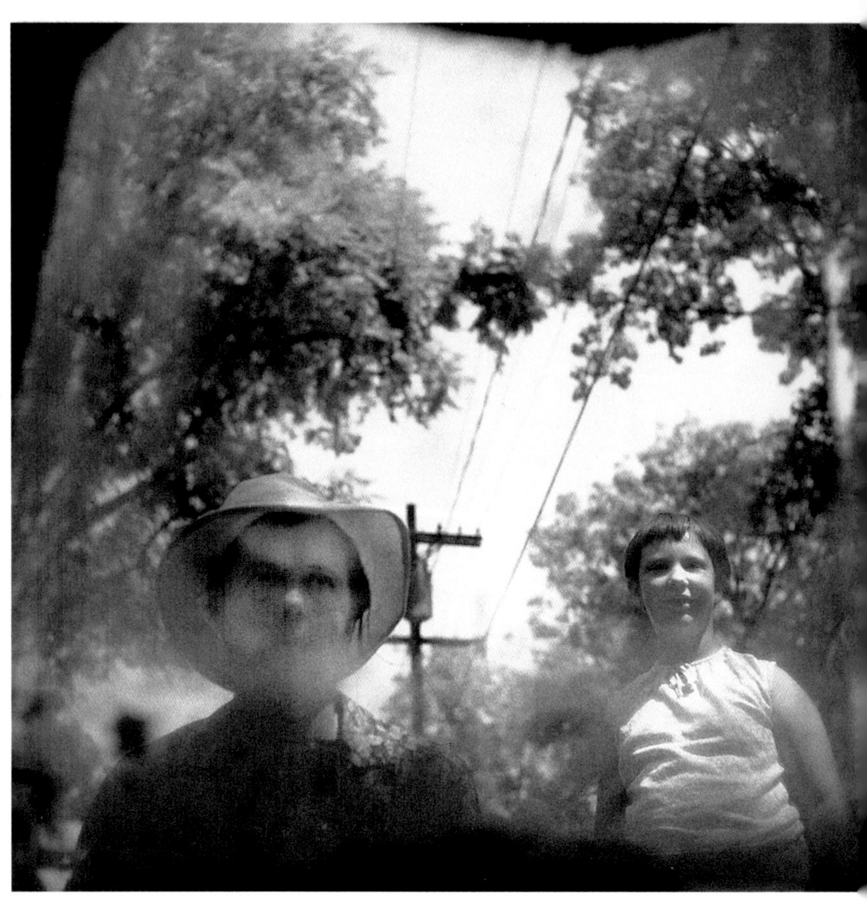

69. Self-portrait, Chicago area, 1970s.

70. 1976.

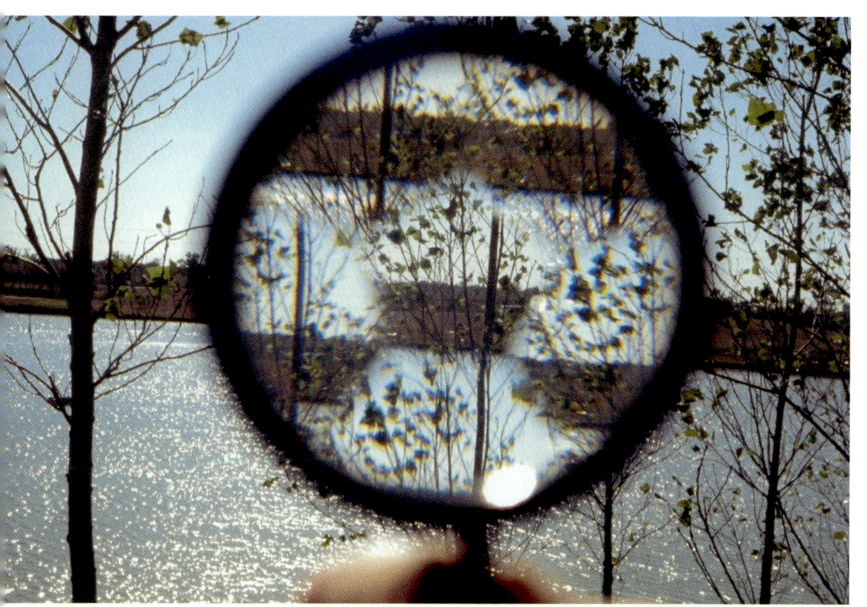

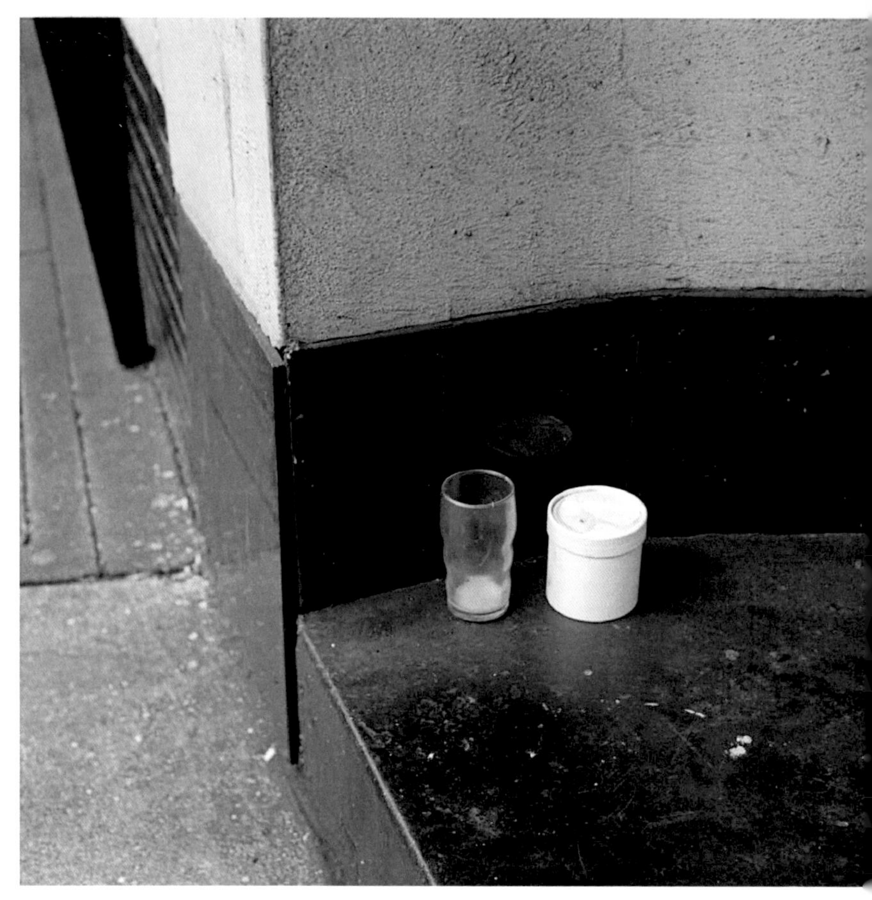

71. Chicago, May 1957.

72. Location and date unknown.

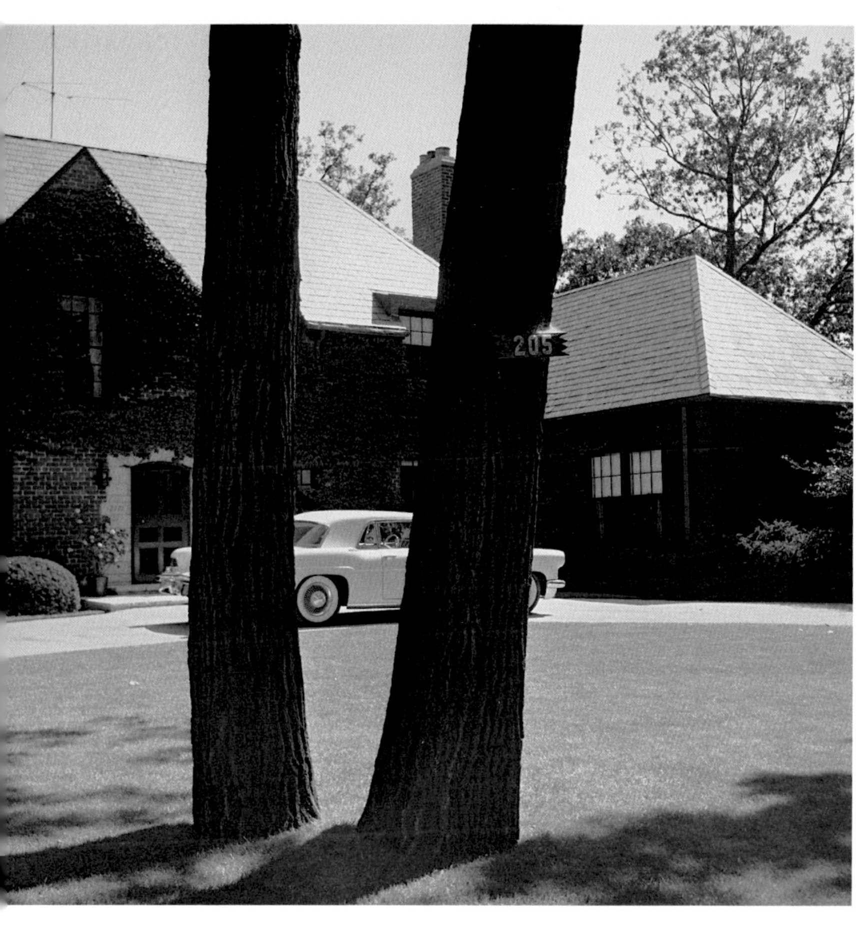
205

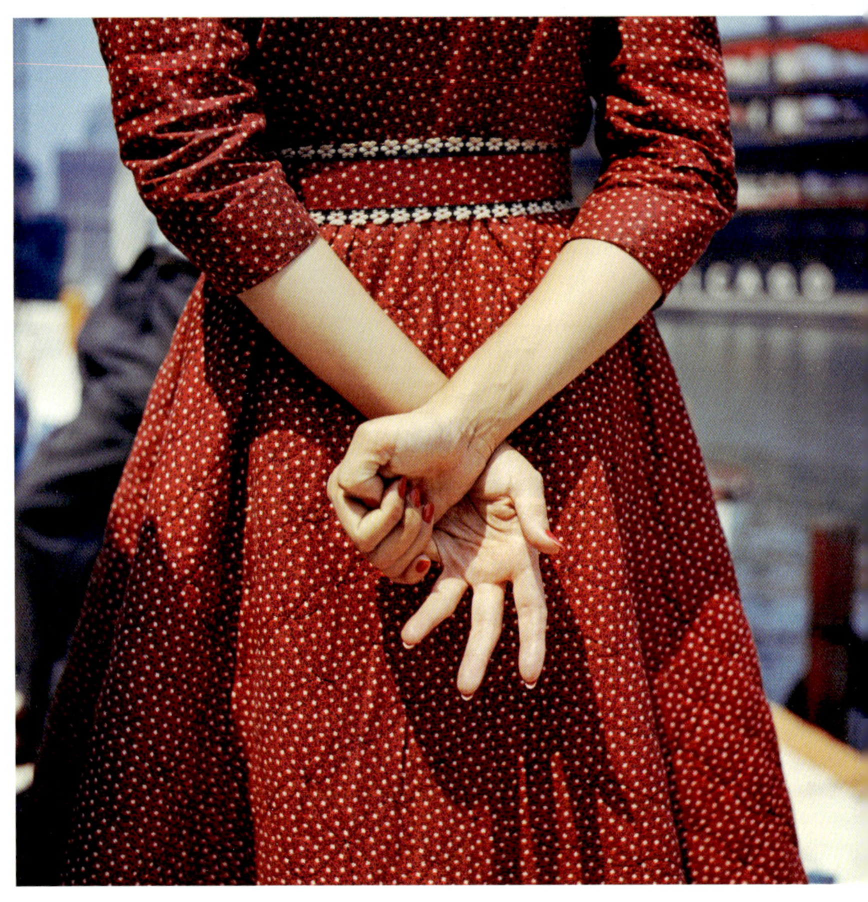

73. 1956.

74. Self-portrait.

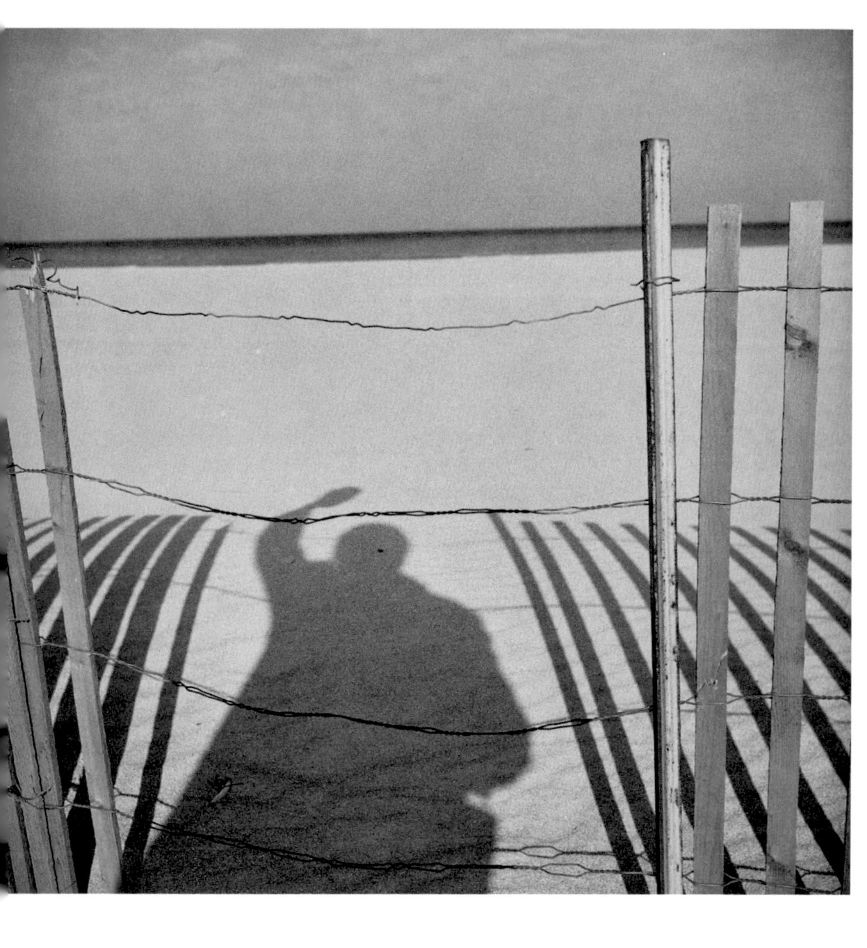

Biography

by Tessa Demichel

1926 Vivian Maier is born in New York on February 1, to a French mother and an Austro-Hungarian father. Her brother Carl, six years older than her, is brought up by his paternal grandparents. The Maiers soon separate.

1930 Vivian and her mother, Maria Jaussaud Maier, move to the Bronx to live with Jeanne Bertrand, a photographer friend who, like them, comes from the French Alps.

1932 They move to France, first to Beauregard, to the family farm of Saint-Julien-en-Champsaur, then to the town of Saint-Bonnet.

1938 Vivian departs for New York on the *Normandie* with her mother, obliged to return to look after Carl, who is about to be released from jail. Vivian, at the age of twelve, is forced to leave her life in the Alps to return to a city she no longer remembers. The family lives on the Upper East Side for a year.

1940s The family splits up completely and Vivian Maier moves to Queens to live with a friend of her maternal grandmother, who becomes her tutor. She gets a job at the Madame Alexander doll factory.

1950 Her great-aunt, Marie-Florentine Jaussaud, dies, designating Vivian as her heir. Vivian's mother is therefore left out of the will and their relationship deteriorates. Vivian Maier decides to sell the Beauregard property and return to France. With a simple box camera, she photographs the Alpine landscapes and takes portraits of local working-class people.

1951 In spring, she leaves France for New York and finds a stable job as a nanny, a flexible role that allows her to spend time outside and take photographs.

1952–1954 In summer 1952, she buys a top-of-the-range Rolleiflex camera. She takes a large number of street photographs and tries, without success, to launch a postcard business, while still working as a nanny.

1955 She travels to the western U.S. via Canada. In the fall, she tours with the Mary Kaye Trio, looking after their children.

1956 She moves to Chicago where she spends eleven years with the Gensburg family in Highland Park. She sets up a small photo lab in her bathroom, where she can develop her negatives and make prints.

1959 She takes a six-month break to go on an around-the-world cruise, with stops in the Philippines, India, China, Yemen, and Europe. Her journey concludes in France; this is her final visit there. She returns from the trip with more than 5,000 photographs.

1960s She becomes interested in filmmaking and acquires two film cameras. She makes many 16 mm and 8 mm films, while continuing to shoot with her Rolleiflex. In some cases, she creates connections between the two mediums, first filming a scene, then photographing it. In the mid-1960s, she begins to move from black and white to color photography, using a Leica 35 mm.

1967 Because the Gensburg children are now grown up, she is obliged to leave the family. In March, she begins a new nanny job with a family in Wilmette, Illinois. She stays there for seven years.

1974 Vivian Maier takes an increasing number of color photographs, taking advantage of the rising popularity and quality of the color film on the market. She gives some of her images to photo laboratories to develop, closely supervising the process.

1975–1980 In the late 1970s, she moves five time in six years, hopping from job to job. Using a tape recorder, she records all kinds of scenes, radio shows, conversations, and shows that she attends. She maintains a prolific photographic output; she roams the streets, watches parades and marches, and goes to film premieres.

1980s She alternates between looking after children and caring for elderly people. She starts putting the old newspapers that she keenly collects into storage, along with her own undeveloped films and prints. Vivian Maier rarely shows her photographs to anyone, even hiding her passion from her employers.

1996 She retires at the age of seventy, which is considered too old to look after young children. She continues to take photographs until 1999, but far less frequently than in the past. The Gensburg children help her find an apartment with a view of Lake Michigan and give her financial support.

2007 Because she can no longer afford to pay for rented storage space, her negatives, prints, audio recordings, and films are sold at auction. John Maloof, who is seeking photographs for a book project on Chicago, buys one of the lots for under $400 and discovers that it's a treasure trove. Vivian Maier's name appears on envelopes from photo labs inside the boxes, but Maloof is unable to trace her. He contacts the other buyers from the auction and gradually recovers the majority of her work.

2009 Following a bad fall, Vivian Maier spends the last few months of her life in a rest home. She dies in Chicago on April 21, at the age of eighty-three. The Gensburg children publish a notice of her death in the *Chicago Tribune* on April 23, describing Vivian Maier as "A free and kindred spirit who magically touched the lives of all who knew her. Always ready to give her advice, opinion, or a helping hand. Movie critic and photographer extraordinaire." John Maloof reads the notice of her death several days after its publication. In October 2009, he publishes Vivian Maier's photographs on the Flickr website, bringing them to public attention for the first time. Her posthumous reputation continues to grow all over the world.

Selected bibliography

Vivian Maier: Street Photographer,
ed. John Maloof, text by Geoff Dyer,
New York: powerHouse Books, 2011
Vivian Maier: Out of the Shadows,
eds. Richard Cahan & Michael Williams,
Chicago: CityFiles Press, 2012
Vivian Maier: Self-Portraits, ed. John Maloof,
New York: powerHouse Books, 2013
Eye to Eye: Photographs by Vivian Maier,
eds. Richard Cahan & Michael Williams,
Chicago: CityFiles Press, 2014
Vivian Maier: A Photographer Found,
eds. John Maloof & Howard Greenberg,
text by Marvin Heiterman & Laura Lippman,
New York: Harper Design, 2014
Vivian Maier: The Color Work, ed. Colin
Westerbeck, text by Joel Meyerowitz,
New York: Harper Design, 2018
Gaëlle Josse, *Une femme en contre-jour*,
Paris: Éditions Noir sur Blanc, 2019
Ann Marks, *Vivian Maier Developed:
The Untold Story of the Photographer
Nanny*, New York: Atria Books 2021
Vivian Maier, ed. Anne Morin, Paris: Réunion
des Musées Nationaux – Grand Palais;
Madrid: diChroma photography, 2021;
London & New York: Thames & Hudson, 2022
Vivian Maier, *Dada* no. 257, 2021
Françoise Perron, *Vivian Maier en toute
discrétion*, Paris: Loco, 2021
Paulina Spucches, *Vivian Maier à la surface
d'un miroir*, Paris: Steinkis, 2021
Arnaud Claass, *Orientations photographiques:
Notes 2020–2022, suivi de Réflexions sur
le cas Vivian Maier*, Paris: Filigranes, 2022
Marion Grébert, *Traverser l'invisible:
Énigmes figuratives de Francesca
Woodman et Vivian Maier*, Strasbourg:
L'Atelier Contemporain, 2022
Émilie Plateau & Marzena Sowa, *Vivian Maier
claire-obscure*, Paris: Dargaud, 2024

Filmography

Jill Nicholls, *Vivian Maier: Who Took Nanny's
Pictures?*, 2013, 70 mins.
John Maloof and Charlie Siskel, *Finding Vivian
Maier*, 2013, 84 mins. Oscar nominee in 2015
for Best Documentary.

Selected exhibitions

2011 Chicago Cultural Center.

2012 Jackson Fine Art, Atlanta.
Vivian Maier: Her Chicago, Chicago History Museum.

2013 *Vivian Maier: Street Life*, Gallery Fifty One, Antwerp.
The Riddle of Vivian Maier, Lumiere Brothers Center for Photography, Moscow.

2014 *Vivian Maier, une photographe révélée*, Jeu de Paume, Tours.

2015 *O mundo revelado de Vivian Maier*, Museu da Imagem e do Som, São Paulo.

2016 *Vivian Maier: In Her Own Hands*, Fundación Foto Colectania, Barcelona.
Vivian Maier: Street Photographer, Fundación Canal, Madrid.
Kulturhuset Stadsteatern, Stockholm.

2017 *Vivian Maier, una fotografa ritrovata*, Palazzo Ducale, Genoa.

2018 *Vivian Maier, la fotógrafa revelada*, Corporación Cultural Las Condes, Santiago de Chile.

2018–2019 *Vivian Maier: Street Photographer*, Art Gallery of Hamilton, Ontario.
Vivian Maier: In Her Own Hands, Willy-Brandt-Haus, Berlin.

2019 *Vivian Maier: A Photographer Revealed*, Kutxa Kultur Artegunea, San Sebastián.
Vivian Maier: The Self-Portrait and Its Double, Magazzino delle Idee, Trieste.

2020 *Vivian Maier: The Self-Portrait and Its Double*, The Finnish Museum of Photography, Helsinki.
Vivian Maier: In Her Own Hands, Glenbow Museum, Calgary.
Vivian Maier: Works in Color, Foam, Amsterdam.

2021 *Finding Vivian Maier*, Today Art Museum, Beijing.

2021–2022 Musée du Luxembourg, Paris.

2022 *Vivian Maier e(s)t son double*, Musée de Pont-Aven; Musée des Beaux-Arts, Quimper.
Bozar, Brussels.
Vivian Maier: Anthology, MK Gallery, Milton Keynes.
Vivian Maier Inedita, Musei Reali, Turin.
Ground Seesaw Seongsu, Seoul.

2024 *Rev(b)elada: Vivian Maier Fotógrafa*, Museo Franz Mayer, Mexico.
Vivian Maier: Unseen Work, Fotografiska Museum, New York.

2024–2025 *Vivian Maier: Anthologie*, Musée de la Photographie Charles Nègre, Nice; Maison des Douanes, Saint-Palais-sur-Mer.

The Photofile series is the original English-language edition of the Photo Poche collection. It was first published between 1986 and 1992 by the Centre National de la Photographie, Paris, with the support of the French Ministry of Culture. Robert Delpire (1926–2017) was the creator of the series and its managing editor until 2017.

General editors: Géraldine Lay and Anne Morin
Assistant editor: Marie Constant

Series design by Matthew Young

Translated from the French by Jill Phythian

Reprinted 2025

First published in the United Kingdom in 2024 by
Thames & Hudson Ltd, 181A High Holborn, London WC1V 7QX

First published in the United States of America in 2024 by
Thames & Hudson Inc., 500 Fifth Avenue, New York, New York 10110

EU Authorized Representative: Interart S.A.R.L.
19 rue Charles Auray, 93500 Pantin, Paris, France
productsafety@thameshudson.co.uk
www.interart.fr

A CIP catalogue record for this book is available from the British Library

Library of Congress Control Number 2024940137.

ISBN 978-0-500-41128-5
02

Printed and bound in Italy

Be the first to know about our new releases, exclusive content and author events by visiting
thamesandhudson.com
thamesandhudsonusa.com
thamesandhudson.com.au